Whatever Became of Salvation?

WHATEVER BECAME OF SALVATION?

JAMES R. BULLOCK

John Knox Press
ATLANTA

Acknowledgments

Scripture quotations are from the Revised Standard Version of the Holy Bible, copyright, 1946, 1952, and © 1971, 1973 by the Division of Christian Education, National Council of the Churches of Christ in the U.S.A. and used by permission.

T. S. Eliot, "Journey of the Magi" in COLLECTED POEMS 1909–1962. Used by permission of Harcourt, Brace, Jovanovich, publishers, New York.

From WHATEVER BECAME OF SIN? by Karl Menninger, M. D. Copyright 1973 by Karl Menninger, M. D. By permission of Hawthorn Books, Inc. All rights reserved.

From AFTER THE FALL by Arthur Miller. Copyright 1964 by Arthur Miller. By permission of The Viking Press, Inc. Publishers, New York.

From WAIT UNTIL EVENING by Henrietta Buckmaster. Used by permission of Harcourt, Brace, Jovanovich, publishers, New York.

From THE WHOLE WORLD IS WATCHING by Mark Gerzon. Copyright 1969 by Mark Gerzon. Used by permission of The Viking Press, Inc., Publishers, New York.

From SMALL IS BEAUTIFUL by E. F. Schumacher. Used by permission of Harper and Row, Publishers, Inc., New York.

From A MAN FOR ALL SEASONS by Robert Bolt. Copyright 1960, 1962 by Robert Bolt. Used by permission of Random House, Inc. Alfred A. Knopf, Inc., Publishers, New York.

From AS WE ARE NOW by May Sarton. Used by permission of W. W. Norton and Company, Inc. Publishers, New York.

Library of Congress Cataloging in Publication Data

Bullock, James R.   1910-
    Whatever became of salvation?

    1. Salvation. I. Title.
BT751.2.B84   234   78-71049
ISBN 0-8042-1468-9

© 1979 John Knox Press
    Atlanta, Georgia

Printed in the United States of America

To my wife, whose "faith, hope and love"
made this book possible

Contents

Whatever Became of Salvation?

Preface

Two ministers were heard talking in a hospital elevator. One spoke of a young man who was "saved" two weeks before. Evidently this was understood as an isolated event, a radical transformation of that individual. What had happened to the man? Had he simply made a decision which was to have important consequences? Had he experienced a total change of life? Or had he embraced certain beliefs which presumably would effect a change? Did it mean all this and much more?

What is salvation? It means many things to many people, depending on their circumstances and desires. For a person reared in the Christian faith it may be a mighty act of God in which an individual becomes a new person, with different ideas and goals, a different attitude toward life, a different way of dealing with fellow human beings as a result of his faith in a Savior. But is it a present possession or a future gift? Does it include the whole process or is it the reward at the end of it? Is it confined to the individual or is it also concerned with the world of which he is a part? Is it for time or eternity or both?

In a broad sense salvation means hope for all kinds of people. Those beyond the Christian fold may long for a change in their world or in themselves. People subject to bondage or oppression of all sorts, people who have known frustration or despair long for some kind of deliverance. We grow tired of failure, disgusted with out own conduct and wonder if there is reason to hope that life may be different.

Does this persistent hope of humanity have any foundation?

On a wall in Northern Ireland there were written these words, "Is there life before death?" The same words could be written on walls in many places throughout the world. The strife in Ireland is a microcosm of the alienation which afflicts all humanity. Can the world be saved from self-destruction? Is there any evidence that salvation is possible?

Those interested in salvation often seem concerned with formulas, theories and experiences which have little bearing on the reality sought—the truly good life, made possible through the grace of God. Despite all evidence to the contrary there is a longing for real goodness. Can it be satisfied?

It is a great pity that in the face of such desperate need Christians have had a hard time coming to some sort of agreement about the nature of salvation. Christ said that he came "not to condemn the world, but that the world might be saved" through him. Salvation is the reason for the existence of the Christian faith, but when Christians come to defining what this involves there is vast disagreement. Ideas are blurred, indistinct. Worse still, these varied conceptions divide Christians and make it difficult for them to work together. The mission of the church and the task of evangelism are in dispute largely because of these differences. A re-examination of the richness and breadth of the biblical conception of salvation may give us a working basis on which we may build a more faithful response to God's work of redemption. This is the hope of the pages that follow.

The writing of this book has been a long journey during which the various themes treated have been thought through many times. Experiences over a lifetime have shed light which a rational analysis failed to give. I am grateful to the many Christian persons who appear in these pages, people who have made contributions to my life and thought through their lives. The book would have been impossible without them. There are countless others among the people I have tried to serve who are not mentioned, but whose help has been invaluable. My special thanks are due to Dick Ray, the editor of John Knox Press, who first suggested this writing and later gave the guidance and suggestions which have produced it in its present form. I am grateful also to other members of the staff of John Knox Press, and to my secretary, Sarah Rudder, whose typing and other help has been most valuable.

CHAPTER ONE

How Real Is Salvation?

Some years after leaving a pastorate in New Orleans we stopped by briefly to visit old friends and attend the church we had served for seven years. After the Sunday morning service we talked with some of the members about those who had been very close to us in the church. We mentioned Miss Charlie Belle, a seamstress who kept the nursery of the church for decades. She was seldom able to attend church services herself, but her loving care of their children enabled countless young parents to attend. During a depression time when the minister's salary was so low that an occasional wedding or funeral fee kept food in our house, she sat with our children in the evening without pay when we had to go out. She did this for a succession of ministers as a service to her church. She had no relatives, but it spoke well of her that a family kept her in its home like a valued grandmother as long as she lived. She had died shortly before our visit and we all mourned her loss.

"Did you ever hear the story of how she made the news in New Orleans in a bus incident?" asked a friend. We had heard nothing of it.

"One evening in the 1950s," said the friend, "Miss Charlie Belle was riding a bus into the city and a young black woman entered. Since the seats at the back were all taken, she took a seat at the front of the bus rather than stand. You remember at that time the buses were segregated for seating and it was against the law for her to sit in the front. The driver tried to make the black woman stand in the rear, but she refused and kept her seat. He became abusive and threatened to remove her bodily. Miss Charlie Belle stood it as long as she could and then rose and defended the woman against the driver. He drove immediately to the police station where the black woman was charged with unlawful trespass. Miss Charlie Belle remained with her to lend support and comfort."

The story was a revelation to us of the depths of kindness and courage in a humble Christian person. She was made of sterner stuff than we imagined. Her action was a portent of greater things to come. We could say of her, "The meek shall inherit the earth."

Someone once said that he would believe in Christianity if he could find a real Christian. Perhaps he would have recognized one on the bus that night. Was he looking for some perfect individual, conforming in every way to the spirit of Christ? It is doubtful that he could find such a person. Outward appearances do not give the full story about anyone, certainly not about Miss Charlie Belle. Self-righteousness, a parade of virtue, would be no qualification. It has problems with pride and self-deceit. Miss Charlie Belle would have been the last to make any claim to goodness in her brave defense of a stranger. She never mentioned it to us. Yet the evident goodness of the woman, the faith and love that made her forget her own safety and risk danger to aid a victim of discrimination, said that something had happened to her and was still happening, something we call salvation. It involved her whole life, all relationships, including those with strangers and the community.

Does our conception of salvation represent adequately what God is doing in and through human beings in the world? Salvation comes in many varieties, through the responses in life of many different kinds of persons. I have known so many people whose reactions in times of testing were undeniably Christian in spite of their obvious weaknesses. Think of a few of these who represent in some fashion multitudes of Christians.

It would be difficult to compare quiet Miss Charlie Belle with the lady we all called Miss Mary although she had been married most of her life. She was a strong, outspoken individual. When she talked you could hear her half a block away. She had pronounced views on most subjects and no hesitation whatever about expressing them. Thin almost to the point of emaciation, she seemed to profit little from her own cooking, but she rejoiced in entertaining others and introduced us to many delectable New Orleans dishes. She had a great sense of humor. She threatened to haunt me if I did not say something good about her at her funeral! Conviviality and good humor represented the lighter side of a loyal and loving person. Whenever there was a death in the church family she was with the bereaved family to comfort them and bring cheer in a way few could match. She could dispel depression and encourage faith in the most despondent, not through repeating pious phrases, but through her own joyous spirit that refused to bow to despair. That same spirit was her strength and comfort through the wasting illness that brought her own death.

Mr. Ed was a leading businessman in our city. We had a corrupt political situation and some of us encouraged him to run for mayor to try to correct it. After prayerful consideration he agreed to do so and won his race. He had to take a large loss in his personal assets as he sold his business to avoid a conflict of interest. He fulfilled his promise to give an honest administration to our city, but he did more. It was at a time when integration of the schools was coming, and he had the vision to see the need for a small beginning. Without a court order, entirely on his own initiative, he had several black children admitted to a junior high school which had previously been all white. He was attacked bitterly, but did not falter in his resolve. As a result he was not returned to office in the next election. He could not be swayed by public pressure either as a city official or as an officer in his church; he made his decisions on the basis of what he felt was right. His integrity commanded the respect of those with whom he disagreed.

Henry was intellectually retarded. For many years he was sheltered by his mother, kept from the world. He rarely spoke to anyone. After his mother died his minister had the insight to ask him to serve his church by picking up the bulletins in the pews after services, distributing literature, offering envelopes, etc., helping with the bulk mailings. It took courage and faith to come out of his shell and learn to meet and serve people, but he managed it. No person could have been more faithful. Through a genuine concern for others he won their affection and admiration. Whenever we had a

visiting speaker he would be one of the first to thank him for coming, introducing himself as a member of the staff, which indeed he
was. His courtesy and kindness spoke of an almost complete self-
forgetfulness. His death was mourned by the whole church.

If we allow our imaginations to function, each of us can think of
many people like these, ordinary people who in some way made
extraordinary responses when challenges came. The personalities and
experiences differ. These people came from different backgrounds of
culture, knowledge and training. Their gifts and contributions varied.
They are as different as two mentioned in the gospels, the rich
Zacchaeus, who agreed to restore all he had taken by fraud and to give
half his goods to the poor after an encounter with Jesus, and the poor
widow whose gift of two small coins was declared by Jesus to be the
largest given to the temple. Each responded in his own way with all
that he had. Jesus declared salvation had come to the house of
Zacchaeus and commended the woman. Salvation is evident in the
human response in faith, love and a certain gallantry to the challenges
of life—discrimination, death, poverty, disease, handicaps. It is the
unexpected response, unexplained save through the inspiration of the
Spirit of God, the work of God's grace.

There are certain likenesses which are impressive in the examples
given. Each of these persons had a faith in God which was a strong
support through a time of testing. Their faith was contagious. It inspired faith in others. It was never a static faith. They ventured out;
with open minds they sought new truth. They had a certain confidence. There is a kind of assurance which turns people away because it implies superiority or overconfidence. In contrast these
people seemed to be undisturbed by the fact that they did not know
all the answers. They were not dogmatic or self-righteous but
seemed to be endowed with a sense of what was the right and loving
action to be taken in each circumstance.

They were all persons for others. In the service of others they
forgot themselves. Their salvation was worked out in personal relationships. Some went further than others in this. Miss Charlie Belle,
acting out of concern for a fellow human being, did something
which helped to initiate a change in an evil system. Ed worked toward the same end in a different way. Each may have been unaware

of the final results of his action. They were products of the Christian fellowship, the church, and were nurtured by it. In turn they were servants of the church and contributed in different ways to its sense of community. Their salvation was a process in which God worked through them toward the salvation of the church and of society.

In each case cited salvation was intensely personal, a reality in an individual life. The conviction that the individual is important lies at the heart of the Christian message. We believe that every person is valued by God. The parables of the lost sheep, the lost coin, the lost son underline this. Jesus was concerned with people of every character, of all ages, from every walk of life. He pointed out that individuals are essential to God's purpose, influential in shaping history. Individual choices make up the pattern of life. When any individuals are neglected all of life suffers.

On the other hand individualism has many dangers. The historian Toynbee made sin equivalent to human egocentricity and his identification has merit. Centering on ourselves can spoil the best things we do. In limiting salvation to the individual our own selfishness can be encouraged. Witness to a relationship with God can become so easily, "Look at what God has done for me." The gospel of success through faith, of a religion that "works," is very appealing; for faith does produce results. However, one wonders if the emphasis on "success" has obscured the real meaning of the gospel of self-forgetful love. How easy it is to confine salvation to the small realm of one's self and shut out the problems of a disturbing world. We enjoy being lulled into a peaceful complacency where nothing disturbs. Some of our hymns tend to encourage this. In reality a person is always a "self-in-the-world," and his life is a constant interplay of self with forces outside—other people, structures of society, the physical world. Our salvation must take all of this into account.

In our tendency to overemphasize the individual aspect of salvation we may ignore its larger dimensions. We sometimes take it for granted that salvation is simply an individual phenomenon. Since the salvation of individuals should lead to results in social life, we reason that these results are secondary, basically derived from individual experiences, and that it is only through individual changes that social changes come. We assume that the primary matter is the salvation of the individual and that all goodness in the common life stems from this. There is no question that the salvation of the individuals described above produces results in the life of society, but this is not the whole story. God's salvation has larger dimensions. It includes both the individual and the group. It extends to all human existence, all human structures.

The Bangkok Conference on *Salvation Today*, held in 1973, included this statement in its message:

> Our concentration upon the social, economic and political implications of the Gospel does not in any way deny the personal and eternal dimensions of salvation. Rather, we would emphasize that the personal, social, individual and corporate aspects of salvation are so interrelated that they are inseparable. . . .

Limiting salvation to individual experiences, as valuable as these are, may incline us to take less seriously the need of the world for the transforming power of God. Walk through the slum districts of a great city and the total degradation of people who live in such an environment is evident. Our news reports depict the destructive conflicts, the heartless acts of violence which destroy humanity. Force is piled on force in vain attempts to make peace through threats and fears. Drug addiction increases. There is an alarming collapse in family life, an eroding of confidence in government through disclosures of corruption and sheer lawlessness in high office. We live in a wasteful fashion in the face of starvation in so much of the world. There is a need for a sensitivity on our part to the agony of the dispossessed, the poor, and the oppressed, and a recognition of what God is doing in his world not only through saved individuals but also through changed social structures to remedy these evils. Recognition should be followed by participation in God's saving work.

Closely akin to the limitation of salvation to the individual's personal experience is a tendency to regard it as exclusively "spiritual," excluding its physical, social, political and economic aspects. The people described at the beginning of this chapter had tremendous spiritual experiences, the guidance of God's Spirit, God's strength to carry them through trying experiences; but their salvation was related to their total life in the world, not an escape from it. Their salvation was not in a compartment separated from the world, uninvolved in "worldly" matters. It is a misconception of the spiritual to think that it refers only to the relationship of a soul of God or to others as individuals. God's Spirit touches all of life. It is the *total* human being who was made in the image of God and who is subject to God in every sphere of his life, who is saved in every aspect of his being.

Similarly, salvation is limited when it is confined to some simple formula. Our credulity and eagerness to grasp at impossible solutions speak of a great need. Unfortunately, there appears to be a lack of comprehension of the real needs of humanity. As a result we are basically naive regarding the answers to the problems involved. Frustrated, anxious, guilt-ridden, we tend to take simplistic answers. An example of such a prescription may run like this: "Give up confidence in your own efforts; trust in Christ for your forgiveness and abundant life for all eternity will be yours." But how much examination is given to what is wrong? The sins confessed may be superficial and the real problem not perceived. "Trust" may be misunderstood. The commitment involved may be vague. "Abundant life" may not be defined at all. The acceptance of the formula may not be accompanied by real change. In our concern for peace of mind we want to be absolutely correct, with the feeling that any deviation from such a course may mean eternal loss. In the process the acceptance of a rigid doctrinal statement may appear to be more important than the rebirth and development of a new person.

It is not surprising that such a limited conception of salvation should appeal to many. There has been a tendency to press Scripture into the mold of a familiar formula. Years ago a speaker at a summer conference gave a series of addresses in which he took the incidents from the Exodus of Israel from Egypt and made them illustrate his idea of the "plan of salvation," identifying parts of the story with election, justification, repentance, faith, baptism, communion, etc.—all applied to individuals. He missed entirely the fact that this was primarily the salvation of a *people* from a condition of bondage for the service of God. It is rather a blatant illustration of a tendency to make God's salvation too small. It is doubtful if the religious experiences of the Christians mentioned earlier could all be described in terms of one formula.

All of those described had a hope of eternal life, although their conceptions of it may have been different. If we confine salvation to this life we miss the significance of the Resurrection. On the other hand, Christianity has suffered from an otherworldliness which makes salvation entirely a matter of the final judgment and ignores its present reality and responsibilities. One church published an evangelistic manual for its workers in which the first question suggested in approaching people about being Christians and church members was, "Can you say for certain that you will go to heaven if death comes today?" The Christians described earlier in this chapter were too busy being followers of Christ to ask themselves such a question or worry about answering it! Later it was asked whether the person approached had heard that Christ delivered from death, that Christ had purchased a place in heaven for him. It was explained that this heavenly acceptance was the really important thing about salvation. Saving faith in Christ had nothing to do with things like health, children, friends, finances, strength for daily living—only with a heavenly home. All that was needed was trust in Christ as Savior and eternal safety was assured. Another church published a set of instructions to be followed with the assurance of a "guaranteed reservation" in heaven for the person accepting the directions!

Perhaps not many would take such a restriction of salvation to another world seriously. The most conservative of Christians see a relevance of the faith to much of everyday life. It is largely a question of emphasis. We can be so absorbed in visions of the future, a heavenly home or even an inner life of contemplation that we become blind to earthly realities and desperate needs of people. It is because we believe that God has a purpose for his world and for humanity that finds its consummation in the future that we also hope for the temporal and provisional. The trouble may be that some folks want release from a world of their own creation, a world that they have misused, rather than a will to change it through the grace of God. Under such circumstances, how real is the prayer, "Thy will be done on earth as it is in heaven"?

It is difficult to avoid the conclusion that when the emphasis in salvation is on personal benefits, on the spiritual as isolated from the secular, on formulas rather than life, and on a world beyond to the exclusion of our present world that some of the most pressing needs of humanity will be neglected. The need for a radical change not only in individuals but also in the society of which they are a part may be ignored. A religion which confines itself to the inner life, which makes few demands, which has no cutting edge can be a pleasant accompaniment to a life directed largely by forces which have nothing to do with faith.

There are no substitutes for dedicated Christian decision and action as illustrated in the lives of those described earlier and multitudes of Christians who are enabled to make a response of faith and love to the challenges life offers. God's gifts come to us under a variety of situations and must be exercised in the real world in which we live. Often weak substitutes for the real thing, active goodness in human life, have placed barriers in the way of fulfillment and have diverted energies which God could have used.

God uses people for the accomplishment of his saving acts, people who respond to his challenge, who make themselves available at the places God is working out his salvation in the world. Some understanding of the dimensions of this salvation may help us to be not only recipients but also instruments of God at the times and places he needs us.

CHAPTER TWO

The Strangeness of God's Mercy

Recently I saw a CBS film about prisons and prisoners. It asked questions about the reasons for incarceration, the treatment of criminals and the process of rehabilitation. One of the men interviewed was imprisoned in a maximum security unit; he was a very dangerous person, convicted of armed robbery. In a cold, emotionless fashion he described his actions and admitted that he would be dangerous on the street. If someone opposed him he would not hesitate to shoot that person. It would be a case of bad judgment on the other's part, not his responsibility. We have difficulty thinking in terms of mercy for a man with so little regard for human life. The question occured to me, "Is the mercy of God extended to such a person?" It is a strange mercy indeed that can forgive and overcome such evil.

Seeing the film reminded me of experiences I had many years before. As a student in the theological seminary I did my "practical work" preaching to the prisoners in the Virginia State Penitentiary in Richmond, teaching some of them in a Bible class, counseling others concerning their problems. As I remember, the prisoners seemed no more cruel, heartless, dishonest or malicious than many people I knew outside the prison walls. There are times when all of us wonder if God's mercy is sufficient to overcome the evil in our lives. Is there a love which can conquer the selfishness and greed which seem to dominate us and to determine most of our decisions?

The rate of crime soars and we are frightened by the threats to our security. We condemn its perpetrators, yet we often acquiesce to the conditions that produce it. A prison official in the film mentioned commented on the fact that the vast majority of criminals came out of conditions of poverty, poor education, inadequate housing, broken homes, unemployment and other evil conditions. Frightened by robberies, cases of rape, and violence of many kinds, we persuade ourselves that stern and violent action is the solution; but such action seems to intensify the atmosphere of violence. It does not go to the root causes. Whenever I hear a judge pronounce a sentence of death on a prisoner and hear those truly dreadful words, "May God have mercy on your soul," I ask the question, "Why have we failed to have mercy on this person?" We fail to eliminate the conditions that produce the crime, at least in some measure, and then attempt to solve the problem by destroying another life. If we believe in the mercy of God, why do we fail to practice it?

The biblical faith affirms that we have a God who cares, who is willing to help, who can save us. There is a strangeness in his mercy, often incomprehensible to us. We find it hard to understand his willingness to save us even when we spurn his help or to accept the fact that his love is greater than human hate and fear. Yet we see it manifested in the cry of Christ from the cross, "Father, forgive them, for they know not what they do." And we read it in the words, "While we were yet sinners Christ died for us."

Some of the problems that affect society as a whole seem so impossible of solution—the economic and political enslavement of peoples in Africa, Latin America, Southeast Asia and elsewhere; the possibilities of mass destruction in war; the threat to our physical environment. Is there a love powerful enough to save us from such disasters?

There is nothing new in all this except, perhaps, the magnitude of the threat. Basically our problems remain the same. In the first chapter of his letter to the Romans Paul described in detail the evils of his time. His account sounds rather contemporary:

> And since they did not see fit to acknowledge God, God gave them up to a base mind and to improper conduct. They were filled with all manner of wickedness, evil, covetousness, malice. Full of envy, murder, strife, deceit, malignity, they are gossips, slanderers,

haters of God, insolent, haughty, boastful, inventors of evil, disobedient to parents, foolish, faithless, heartless, ruthless. Though they know God's decree that those who do such things deserve to die, they not only do them but approve those who practice them. (Romans 1:28–31)

Paul gave no support to the person condemning such evil in the world. The person judging was himself in need of repentance and forgiveness for wrongdoing. Nor did Paul spare himself. In Romans 7:21–24 he writes of his own dilemma:

So I find it to be a law that when I want to do right, evil lies close at hand. For I delight in the law of God, in my inmost self, but I see in my members another law at war with the law of my mind and making me captive to the law of sin which dwells in my members. Wretched man that I am! Who will deliver me from this body of death?

We can identify with this cry for help. We fall far short of real goodness in our attitudes and actions. We can scarcely escape the conclusion that we have a part in the world's evil. Like Isaiah (6:5), we can say:

"Woe is me! For I am lost; for I am a man of unclean lips, and I dwell in the midst of a people of unclean lips. . . ."

Where shall we find help? The Bible is quite clear about the evils which degrade and destroy human beings and their world. There is a candor about the description of wickedness in people and in institutions. The judgment pronounced on such evils and those who perpetrate them is never minimized. Yet throughout the Scriptures there runs a constant theme, that God is determined to save, that he has an unswerving purpose to deliver humanity from evil, and that his power is equal to that purpose. This is true both of the Old Testament and the New.

"If I were the Lord God," wrote Martin Luther in one of his *Table Talks,* "and these vile people were as disobedient as they now be, I would knock the world in pieces." Happily, God is not like Luther. Luther himself, being a man of hope, was not always despairing as in this case. This is God's world. He created it and pronounced it good. If it is twisted and spoiled he intends to restore it. This is the biblical hope.

What is impressive in the Old Testament is the breadth and scope of the salvation for which people hoped. The range of expectation was a wide one. The Hebrew people hoped for deliverance from evil and forgiveness of sins, but they also looked for salvation from sorrows and afflictions, pestilence and death. They prayed for protection from enemies, oppressors, persecutors, liars, the malicious and the wicked. The whole range of human evil, frustration and danger was to be overcome through the love and goodness of God. In the second chapter of 1 Samuel, Hannah, the mother of Samuel, describes her salvation from barenness, and describes other saving works:

> "He raises up the poor from the dust;
> he lifts the needy from the ash heap. . . ."(1 Samuel 2:8)

The writer of Psalm 37 is thankful for another reason:

> The salvation of the righteous is from the LORD;
> he is their refuge in the time of trouble. (Psalm 37:39)

Enlightment was the need of another:

> Lead me in thy truth, and teach me,
> for thou art the God of my salvation. . . . (Psalm 25:5)

Another psalmist sounds a note of rejoicing:

> . . . thou hast delivered my soul from death,
> my eyes from tears,
> my feet from stumbling. (Psalm 116:8)

When David brought the Ark of the Covenant, the central object of the Hebrew worship, to Jerusalem, this prayer was offered for the salvation of the nation:

> "Deliver us, O God of our salvation,
> and gather and save us from among the nations,
> that we may give thanks to thy holy name,
> and glory in thy praise." (1 Chronicles 16:35)

The prophets pictured God as going beyond human expectations in his love for people. As Isaiah 65:1 puts it:

I was ready to be sought by those who did not ask for me;
I was ready to be found by those who did not seek me.
I said, "Here am I, here am I,"
   to a nation that did not call on my name.

There is a strangeness about a mercy like this which we find it
hard to understand, a persistent love, undiscouraged by a lack of
human response, hoping for an answering trust in the future, creat-
ing "new heavens and a new earth."
   It is significant that a nation was addressed most often as the
subject of salvation. The Hebrews never tired of describing their deliverance from Egypt. The salvation they had experienced at the
Red Sea was hailed as the birth of a nation. When they were given
the Ten Commandments at Sinai they were reminded that God had
delivered them from bondage. When they became prosperous they
were not allowed to forget that God had saved them. They were reminded of this in times of triumph as well as in the despairing times
when other nations dominated them. The psalmists and prophets
repeated the refrain. This was not simply a rejoicing over a national
deliverance. They had been saved for the service of God. Their salvation was a part of God's redemptive work in history. They were a
part of a universal salvation. The prophet of the Exile describes
their call:

Thus says God, the LORD,
   who created the heavens and stretched them out,
   who spread forth the earth and what comes from it,
who gives breath to the people upon it
   and spirit to those who walk in it:
"I am the LORD, I have called you in righteousness,
   I have taken you by the hand and kept you;
I have given you as a covenant to the people,
   a light to the nations
   to open the eyes that are blind
to bring out the prisoners from the dungeon,
   from the prison those who sit in darkness.
I am the LORD, that is my name. . . ." (Isaiah 42:5-8)

   This salvation could be described as "a refuge," "a stronghold,"
"a shield," "a support," "a light," "a joy," "a vindication," "a deliverance from enemies." It was a salvation for a people, Israel, and for

individuals. It was primarily a trust rather than a benefit. Salvation was a broad concept, covering all of human life—moral, social, political, economic, physical and spiritual. The passages above testify to this. It was the help and favor of God that made life bearable as well as making it acceptable to God.

How has God saved man? The writers of the Old Testament saw God as acting in behalf of his people, intervening in times of oppression or strife, raising up gifted leaders, delivering from individual distress. The prophets saw God as stirring up leaders outside Israel, like Cyrus of Persia, to give freedom and opportunity to Israel. The forgiveness and restoration of the sinner was a part of God's redemption. The New Testament centers around God's act in sending Christ to identify with sinful humanity and become its Savior. The Bible shows that we may understand God's power and intention to save through images, figures of speech which help us to understand his action on our behalf.

A picture which grows out of the experience of a people who herded sheep is that of a shepherd. "The LORD is my shepherd," writes the psalmist, describing God's care for his people in terms of a shepherd's care for the flock. This picture of God's redemption in terms of loving care is used by Isaiah, Ezekiel and others in the Old Testament. In the New Testament Jesus describes himself as the Good Shepherd.

This picture is not a familiar part of life to most of us, but it suggests an answer to many of our human needs which comes through the work of God in our lives. The work of the shepherd is suggestive of God's ministry to human need for comfort and care. As the shepherd tended his flock in a barren land where it was difficult to find food and water, so God provides for our human needs in a world of difficulties. Sometimes he works through others. I see God's saving love in the work of an older man who has cared for his arthritic wife through many years. Cooking, cleaning, nursing, he has made it possible for her to live in her own home rather than having to endure the loneliness of a nursing home. Our human compassion finds its inspiration in the the loving care of God.

As the shepherd guided and protected his flock, so God answers our need for guidance and protection. The shepherd protected his sheep from wild beasts, precarious terrain. He kept them from going astray. So we believe God protects us. We pray, "Lead us not into temptation," and the power to resist is given. We pray, "Deliver us from evil," and evils are averted. Sometimes the inner resources God gives us are sufficient. At other times God works through faithful counselors. Our need is evident:

> All we like sheep have gone astray;
>   We have turned every one to his own way;
> And the LORD has laid on him the iniquity of us all. (Isaiah 53:6)

There is another human need to which this ancient picture of a shepherd suggests a remedy. In a world of multitudes we become lost in the crowd. As lonely persons in a vast sea of humanity it may seem at times that we have little significance. Christ's parable of the shepherd's search for the lost sheep says unmistakably that every person is important in God's sight, that the love of God is available to every human being. It is a sacrificial love in which the shepherd is willing to lay down his life for his sheep. So we never walk alone. A missionary couple in Taiwan was called back to this country recently for the funeral of a young son killed in an automobile accident. In a letter to a friend they said they had never felt alone or deserted.

Salvation is sometimes given a commercial description. In the song of Moses and his people after the crossing of the Red Sea the Israelites are called "the people whom thou hast purchased." Paul uses the same figure in 1 Corinthians 6:19–20: "... You are not your own; you were bought with a price. So glorify God in your body." The picture is of a slave market, with human beings being bought and sold. In the seventh chapter of the same letter Paul encourages slaves to seek their freedom if possible, but particularly to avoid selling themselves into slavery again. "You were bought with a price; do not become the slaves of men." Spiritually they were free, but their new freedom as Christians had a direct bearing on the problem of physical slavery. Christianity had to live with slavery in the early centuries of this era while recognizing it as an evil. For us it is a guilty memory, but it is still a reality in many parts of the world, particularly economic and political slavery. Although he recognized slavery as an evil, Paul was speaking to a broader need of humanity in this parable, the need for freedom from all that holds us in bondage, evil habits and desires, the selfishness that makes us unconcerned about our neighbors. Bondage may be imposed by others or it may be peculiar to our own nature and situation. Somerset Maugham described a particular kind in his novel *Of Human Bondage*—the powerful attraction of a young man to an evil woman.

How shall this freedom come? The picture we have in Scripture suggests that we have been ransomed, that God has purchased our freedom. As Jesus stated it, " . . . the Son of man came not to be served but to serve, and to give his life as a ransom for many" (Matthew 20:28). Christ gave himself for us in sacrificial love upon the cross. That God should sacrifice himself as the cost of our salvation is staggering, beyond our limited comprehension.

The picture has some problems for us. To whom is the ransom paid? To God? This is out of accord with the description in the Scriptures of God as infinite love. Love demands no payment for itself. Is the ransom to be paid to the devil? This brings theological as well as scriptural difficulties. We have to remember that this parable has its limitations.

There is a most important meaning in this parable of the price paid. Self-sacrificial love is costly. Nothing says this in a stronger manner than the life and death of Christ. Countless examples of sacrificial love in human lives say the same thing. Sacrificial love is liberating. It challenges our selfishness on the one hand while assuring us of our individual worth on the other. The unlimited sacrificial love of God has a power to liberate which is lacking in our limited human loves. The commercial picture reveals one facet of this divine love, but there are others.

Our human guilt for wrong done poses a problem. We are torn between our conviction that there is a moral order and we are personally responsible for violating it on the one hand and the intolerable burden of unforgiven sin on the other. How shall our problem be resolved? How shall the moral order be maintained and human beings freed from guilt from violating it? A life without moral standards would be chaotic. Personal responsibility for evil committed gives us dignity as responsible human beings. Dr. Karl Menninger in his book *Whatever Became of Sin?* argues rightly that much is lost in losing sight of personal sin, making people who err either patients or public lawbreakers. Sin needs to be considered as a serious break between ourselves and God, ourselves and others; but what can be done about it? How shall the guilt of such ruptures be erased?

In his letter to the Romans Paul presents a picture which suggests a remedy. The scene is a law court in which God is the judge. Human beings are found guilty of wrong and stand condemned. The law is upheld strictly. Penalties are imposed. Into this court there steps one who takes the punishment for the guilty. It is "... Jesus our Lord, who was put to death for our trespasses and raised for our justification" (Romans 4:24–25). The Judge himself, who is guiltless, takes the place of the condemned. We are "justified by faith" by accepting what Christ has done for us. The righteousness of which we were incapable becomes ours through faith in Christ.

This parable of judgment states unmistakably that evil is abhorrent to God and that he desires good in human beings, but this is not the end of the matter. The chief thrust of the parable is that retribution is not God's final answer to the sin of human beings. Suffering, corruption, degradation often follow evil; but it is not always the perpetrators of evil who suffer its consequences. When retribution does overtake evildoers it is scarcely an instrument of reformation. It destroys rather than saves. The great truth of this picture of God's judgment is that there is something stronger than retribution that overcomes sin, the self-sacrificial love of God.

The parable also says that human beings are incapable of saving themselves. The prophets of the Old Testament, Jeremiah and Ezekiel, recognized both the individual and corporate responsibility for sin. They saw their people's salvation in a return to obedience to the laws of God. Unfortunately, their attempts at perfect fulfillment were unsuccessful and led to a self-righteousness that was destructive. Jesus condemned it in the Pharisees. Paul found self-reformation impossible and came through long experience to the conclusion that God alone can make us righteous. Human resources alone are insufficient. The parable of judgment assures us that we have resources, supplied through Christ, to make goodness a reality in our lives.

A part of our problem is that we have an inadequate understanding of the justice of God and pattern our moral lives on this misunderstanding. Our idea of justice may be the achievement of equity, like treatment for everyone, fairness in all things. This is good as far as it goes, but God goes beyond this. In his strange mercy he loves and saves the undeserving as well as those who come closer to the mark. Equal treatment is superseded by second-mile love and care.

Again our misunderstanding may be an overemphasis on justice as retribution. We sometimes think a person receives justice when he is judged fairly and "the punishment fits the crime." Some endeavor to combine the "eye for an eye and tooth for a tooth" conception of justice in the Old Testament with the New Testament teaching of forgiveness through the grace of God. This is done by making salvation quite separate from our administration of justice in the secular realm. If salvation is relevant to all life this is an impossible separation. Jesus said that the "eye for an eye and tooth for a tooth" philosophy no longer held for his followers. He encouraged us to love our enemies, not to punish them.

The parable of judgment says that love overcomes retribution. We may be thinking, in our zeal for righteousness, that God is first of all a just God and only secondarily loving and forgiving. This is not the proper order. The Scriptures teach that God's righteous judgments are a part of his saving activity, that there is no conflict between justice and love, that in the last analysis they are the same. Shakespeare in *The Merchant of Venice* has Portia say in her famous defense speech, "earthly power doth then show likest God's when mercy seasons justice." Mercy does more. It informs and empowers justice. It makes justice possible in a world where we continually judge each other and seek to destroy each other. It heals and restores rather than destroys and rejects.

There is one last picture of this determined love of God to save human beings, this strange mercy. It comes from the sacrificial system of the temple in the Old Testament era in which animals were slain and burned upon an altar in order that sins might be forgiven.

It expressed a deep need for forgiveness for evil. It is difficult for us to see how the death of animals could have any connection with forgiveness, other than the sacrifice involved in giving the animals for that purpose. Such a system is remote to us, even repulsive. In fact the system was often abused, used as a way of "bargaining with God," as a means for temple authorities to enrich themselves, as a substitute for real goodness. The prophet Hosea expressed God's judgment on this:

> ... I desire steadfast love and not sacrifice,
> the knowledge of God, rather than burnt offerings.
> (Hosea 6:6)

Nonetheless this ancient system had deep symbolic meaning for the writers of the New Testament. Through its reference to Christ on the cross it spoke of a sacrificial love of God which satisfied the human need for forgiveness and peace with God. The writer of Hebrews adopted this imagery to explain the reason why Christ became man to save us:

> Therefore he had to be made like his brethren in every respect, so that he might become a merciful and faithful high priest in the service of God, to make expiation for the sins of the people. For because he himself has suffered and been tempted, he is able to help those who are tempted. (Hebrews 2:17–18)

The picture given in Hebrews is of the priest who offers himself as the sacrifice:

> ... he entered once for all into the Holy Place, taking not the blood of goats and calves but his own blood, thus securing an eternal redemption. (9:12)

So Christ gave himself, once for all, "to bear the sins of many." Its great appeal is the revelation of a self-giving love of God which calls us to self-giving. Paul used it in this fashion in his letter to the Ephesians:

> Therefore be imitators of God, as beloved children. And walk in love, as Christ loved us and gave himself up for us, a fragrant offering and sacrifice to God. (Ephesians 5:1–2)

The challenge is even stronger in the letter to the Romans:

I appeal to you therefore, brethren, by the mercies of God to present your bodies as a living sacrifice, holy and acceptable to God, which is your spiritual worship. (Romans 12:1)

Engrossed in our own pursuits, seeking satisfaction for our own desires, we become oblivious to the needs of others. Self-sacrifice observed in others challenges us. Dedicated lives, even imperfect ones, call us to self-forgetfulness. But it is the infinite love of God in Christ which is powerful enough to deliver us from the tyranny of self.

All these pictures of God's saving activity say that God really cares about humanity. Each emphasizes some different aspect of that love and some human need met. God cares enough to condemn the evil that destroys. He is not satisfied with twisted and perverted lives. He is willing to go beyond human expectation, to pay the ultimate cost, to identify with us completely in order to save us, to give us abundant life. In his incarnation Christ accomplished all this. The writer of Hebrews calls him "the pioneer of our salvation," not ashamed to call us brethren, able to help us because he shared our suffering and temptation.

Is there any other explanation of redemption than that of a persistent, determined love that never gives us up, that changes all it touches? God loved a wayward people in the Old Testament period and that love reclaimed them again and again. In Christ that love reaches its climax and perfection. "God so loved the world that he gave his only Son." In a world that often discourages us, where human evil reaches appalling depths, it is the love of God that supports us and gives hope, a love without limitations. Graham Greene in a number of his novels has endeavored to explore the depth and breadth of that divine love through characters obviously human but with an uncommon urge to practice sacrificial love. In *Brighton Rock* he pictures a young girl who loves an incredibly evil man who tries to kill her. So great is her love that she is willing to be condemned with him. When she communicates this feeling to a priest he is sensitive to the depths of her love. He tells her the story of a man who loved humanity so much that he identified with it in its wretchedness and damnation. The priest thought there was hope for him in the love of God, as there was for her. "You can't conceive, my child, nor can I or anyone–the . . . appalling . . . strangeness of the mercy of God. It was a case of greater love hath no man than this, that he lay down his soul for his friend."

In her tender novel about old age, *As We Are Now,* May Sarton describes a lonely old woman in a nursing home who has found someone to love. She writes in her diary, " . . . this is one of the proofs of true love. It always comes as revelation, and we approach it always with awe as if it had never taken place before on earth in any human heart, for the very essence of its power is that it makes all things new" (p. 98). This is what happens to those who know the redeeming love of God. The capacity to love is born out of being loved.

CHAPTER THREE

A Life Renewed

A telephone call came on a recent evening. It was a woman telling me of her brother-in-law's serious heart attack. The comforting power of faith was needed in addition to all the measures being used to save him physically. When I reached the hospital I found the man doing well, the result of swift attention to his needs. The family described what happened when the attack came. Happily, a nurse had been in the room and observed his condition. She called out a code number over the intercom and within seconds there were specialists on the scene to do what was necessary to save his life, including the installation of a temporary pacemaker. Life is valuable. We spare no effort or expense to save it.

We hear of a child who has fallen into a deep well and we listen with impatience for news of his rescue because we can identify with his struggle for life. The same process takes place when we learn of miners trapped under the earth in an explosion or cave-in. A noted statesman dies and thousands file by his casket to pay tribute to his life and mourn his loss. Much of the sorrow we manifest is for ourselves, for the fact that we also are mortal. Our sorrow shows how we value life.

What is this human life which we value so highly? Is it merely our biological existence, a more complex, more highly organized form of the life than we observe in plants and animals, and nothing more? Is it no more than a "walking shadow," a "brief candle" soon to be snuffed out, as Shakespeare's Macbeth imagined it (Act V, Sc. 5)? Such a conception gives no explanation of human reason, of "faith, hope and love," of the reaching out of the human spirit. We can reflect on our past and be concerned about our future. We are aware that life must be something more than physical existence. The "quality of life" is a subject of discussion in some of our cities. Usually this means the physical and intellectual conditions under which people live. Life is considered good if people live in decent homes and have good air to breathe, clean water, ample nutrition, medical care, recreational opportunities, intellectual stimulation, proper schools, adequate protection from the hazards of crime, fire, traffic accidents, etc. Each of us can make his own list. Make no mistake! All these things are very important. When they are absent life is impoverished. The person who works for adequate housing or participates in a "meals on wheels" program, taking hot meals to those unable to prepare food for themselves, is making a very real contribution to the "abundant life" which is God's will for humanity. Efforts now being made in many parts of the world to bring economic justice to millions of poor people are very real contributions to the enrichment of life. But life goes beyond environment, beyond provision for basic needs such as those described above.

Is life to be measured in terms of possessions? Possessions do enhance life, make it interesting, provide opportunities. Ownership can be a tool for the development of character. Possessions enable us to have independence and exercise creativity, but they have certain liabilities. Most of us cannot resist the temptations of seeking possessions for the power they give us or the pleasure of accumulation. Possessions become idols that motivate us. We are tempted to measure life in terms of property and the prestige it confers. We defer to those most successful in the world of business, sports, entertainment, etc. and seek to emulate them. An advertisement in a magazine a few years ago had this line, "You are in a new age of accumulation." We are urged to acquire things we may not use while the majority of the people of the earth lack even the basic necessities of existence. Considering all this we can see why Jesus said, " . . . a man's life does not consist in the abundance of his possessions" (Luke 12:15). Everything depends upon the use of possessions, whether they become the means of self-aggrandizement or

tools of loving service. Life must be something more than possessions which may be a temptation to us and which we enjoy for such
a limited time.

Is pleasure or excitement the measure of life? Surely the search
for beauty and its enjoyment enlarges life. In one of his brighter
moments Ecclesiastes, the preacher of the Old Testament, wrote of
humanity (3:12–13):

> I know that there is nothing better for them than to be happy and
> enjoy themselves as long as they live; also that it is God's gift to
> man that everyone should eat and drink and take pleasure in all
> his toil.

Unfortunately this writer was more often pessimistic about human
life, but he could see that there is nothing wrong in human joy.
Jesus was a joyful person, taking pleasure in social gatherings, helping to make a wedding a joyous occasion. He wanted his joy to be in
his disciples (John 15:11). All of life can be a joyous adventure
through the pursuit of our various interests and enthusiasms and the
use of all our creative abilities so long as we remember that being
amused is not the chief end of life. The trouble about making our
own pleasure the goal of living is that we run out of experiences that
are fascinating enough to excite us. The same can be said for our
search for popularity or power. Life does not find its complete
meaning in what we have, how we are regarded or how we influence
others. All these bring the temptation to center in one's self and forget the needs of others. Each falls short of making life ultimately
meaningful.

The fact is that we may have more possessions than we know
how to use, be admired by multitudes, be able to do almost anything we please, and still be afraid of life. The externalities of our
existence do not seem to equip us to face its realities with faith and
hope. The more we shrink from the problems of life the more worth-
less we feel ourselves to be. Our earthly history becomes a series of
humiliating retreats until we reach the place where no retreat is possible. We fear life because we fear death. We are unwilling to take
any risk which might disturb our fancied security, so life becomes

immobilized and eventually fades away. We need help, liberation from an existence haunted by fears.

Some of us react in a different fashion. We picture ourselves as indomitable. We may think that we are equal to every problem and every strain in our own strength. This illusion of superiority covers up the sure and deeply buried knowledge that we are mortal and fallible. Yet we refuse to admit this. We are fearful of standing helpless and vulnerable before the world and of risking the inner despair of such a revelation. We sometimes turn to destructive measures to prove superiority, to preserve the image. So Saul persecuted the early Christians because they represented a threat to his self-esteem and to the system on which he had built his whole life.

This same Saul, who became Paul, wrote of another familiar problem, moral failure. In the seventh chapter of Romans he describes his experience, his personal inability to live a life of legal perfection. We can identify with that for we share his conflict. We know what is right. We desire to do it, but there is something perverse inside us which defeats our good intentions. Paul felt enslaved by his own evil and cried out, "Who will deliver me from the body of this death?" He found forgiveness and peace through ceasing to trust in his own efforts and placing his confidence in Christ. Instead of relying on obedience to a written law to save him, he found a new source of goodness. He wrote to the Romans, " ... the law of the Spirit of life in Christ Jesus has set me free from the law of sin and death" (8:2). It was a gift of God, a new life made possible through the work of God's Spirit. For him it came in a shattering experience on the road to Damascus, probably growing out of inner conflict and followed by a long period of growing understanding of what had happened to him. For many of us it comes in different ways. For all of us it is an experience of renewal by a power beyond ourselves, a renewal that touches all of life.

What kind of life is this which is an answer to our urgent need, which brings victory over fear, anxiety, pride, moral failure? It is a life of faith, of trust in God. It is "the assurance of things hoped for, the conviction of things not seen," as the writer of Hebrews expressed it. The eleventh chapter of that letter describes those who lived through such a faith. They are described as "seeking a home-land," desiring "a better country." Life is poor indeed when there is no vision of the future, no zest to seek new truth, no resources but human ones to combat the evil and despair which engulf us. I think of one who found a triumphant faith. She suffered from a fatal disease. Those who cared for her were saddened by the spectacle of her suffering, but they were inspired by her gallant fight against the malady. She never gave up. She attempted to carry on her work in spite of constant pain. Like the heroes of faith described in Hebrews 11:39, she did not receive what was promised in this life. But through a strong faith in Christ she looked forward to a fulfillment in the future. Just as those men and women of faith in Hebrews inspired others who came after them, so her faith was an inspiration to those she touched.

This renewed life must involve moral decision, responding to the obligations and responsibilities we face before God. The sermon of Moses in Deuteronomy 30 sets forth the alternatives which faced the Hebrew people as they entered a new land to build a new life:

> ... I have set before you life and death, blessing and curse; there-fore choose life that you and your descendants may live, loving the LORD your God, obeying his voice, and cleaving to him. . . . (Deuteronomy 30:19–20)

This was more than an obligation to obey a set of rules. It was a call to a new role as a people of God responsive to his leading. Unfortunately their subsequent history displayed a tendency to choose death more often than life, rebelling against God rather than loving and serving him. Their experience as a nation demonstrated that life must have a moral purpose to be meaningful. It must be a life under God. C. S. Lewis tells of walking over a bridge at Oxford one evening and hearing the conversation of two young people underneath it.

"Do you love me?" asked the boy.
"Under God," was the reply.

Lewis thought that under that condition their life together had high hope for success. Whenever we resolve to live "under God" in business or any profession or work or in the home, the political arena or the social sphere, then life is different, utterly new in its motivation and its outworkings.

We can measure this new life in terms of relationships with others, loving relationships which build life. We are self-deceived if we consider ourselves better able to manage without others. We are fortunate if we learn that the need of other people is essential to life's fulfillment, even more fortunate if we find that others need us. Human affection is a necessity. Life is stunted without it. Life is made meaningful by all sorts of people, those who challenge us as well as those who support us.

Relationships, unfortunately, can be perverted. Tragedies are created by those who desire to possess others—husbands, wives, children, friends, associates, employees. Domination destroys life. Relationships have their dangers, but they extend life beyond the individual. We live most fully as we live with others.

As a pastor I must confess that there are many days when making pastoral calls is something I do not like to face. There may be homes involved where people are distant, uninterested or even hostile. There are so many things I would rather do in my study, safely insulated from people. So I have to force myself to go out and knock on doors. Whenever this happens I have surprises in store for me. Those I visit contribute more to me than I do to them. New understandings come. I go to comfort and am comforted. Life is made richer and fuller through relationships of trust, concern and interest we share with others.

This new life involves responsibilities to neighbors, to all who touch our lives. A lawyer came to Jesus and asked the question, "Teacher, what shall I do to inherit eternal life?" (Luke 10:25–37). He was told that the observance of the great commandments of love to God and neighbor was the answer. When the question of the identity of the neighbor was asked the answer was given in the story of the Good Samaritan. Eternal life is realized in neighborliness. It is essentially a new relationship to our fellows based upon a new relationship to Christ.

John's testimony in his gospel and in his first letter is that eternal life is essentially life in Christ. "In him was life, and the life was the light of men" (John 1:4). In response to those who criticized his healing on the sabbath, Jesus spoke of his works as bearing witness to him as one sent of God to bring life. His way of life, his service of his fellows, his response to human need give us guidelines for life. He spoke of the testimony of the Scriptures to him: "You search the scriptures because you think that in them you can have eternal life; and it is they that bear witness to me; yet you refuse to come to me that you may have life ... " (John 5:39–40). He challenges us just as he did these people of long ago and the challenge demands a response of faith. The new life which he offers becomes a reality for us as we put trust in him. He is the wellspring of our lives. As Paul wrote to the Colossians in a mystical vein, he *is* our life. The Christian life is none other than Christ's incarnate life in the world. Life eternal is to know God as he really is, as we know him in Christ. It is to grasp his unselfishness, generosity, patience, humility and love as we identify with him. As he prayed for his disciples, " ... this is eternal life, that they know thee, the only true God, and Jesus Christ whom thou hast sent" (John 17:3).

What does it mean to "know" Christ? Knowing about him is more than intellectual knowledge. It implies a living fellowship in which his love takes over and our inability to love is overcome. Knowing Christ may come in many ways, through unusual experiences, the making of decisions, the understanding of friends, insights from God's word, the fellowship of prayer.

Elizabeth Yates has written a short novel, *The Carey Girl*, a simple but profound story of a girl who lost interest in living because of rejection by a man she loved and so took poison to end her life. The poison was phosphorus which acted slowly, entering her tissues to destroy her. After it was too late she discovered that she did not want to die. She was aided by a kind doctor and his wife with whom she discovered the meaning of life. Her life had been stunted by a broken home and rejection by her parents, which resulted in a personality incapable of love. Through concerned and loving people she found a happiness which her pain was unable to touch. Through their faith and hope, their communication of the love of God in Christ, she found faith and hope for herself. Through her suffering love was born. She found life, which is really the freedom of the spirit to love, unhampered by the artificial barriers which we set up in our human folly, a life not subject to death.

This eternal life is essentially a new quality of life. Christ emphasized this in several parables. One was about new wine that could not be placed in old bottles lest it burst them; another about new cloth that could not be sewed successfully to an old garment. The life he brought could not be confined in old customs and ways of thought. It was radically different, so different that Nicodemus was told that he must be born again to experience it, that there must be a complete change in his attitudes and actions. Paul speaks of it as walking "in newness of life" (Romans 6:4), experiencing a "new life of the Spirit" (Romans 7:6). He described this life to the Ephesians as a "new nature, created after the likeness of God in righteousness and holiness" (Ephesians 4:24) and to the Colossians as "the new nature, which is being renewed in knowledge after the image of the Creator" (Colossians 3:10). These expressions picture a dynamic change in human life, a process of change initiated and carried on by God.

Such a life is a gift of God. All of life, for that matter, is a gift. Sometimes it takes a dramatic experience to make us recognize it. Anne Morrow Lindbergh in *The Steep Ascent* tells of going with her husband from England to Italy in a small plane many years ago. She was expecting a child but was determined to make the trip. The crossing of the Alps through difficult passes was a tense experience. They ran into cloud banks on the Italian side, lost their way and narrowly missed striking a mountain in their descent. It was a frightening experience for all, but with the release from danger there came the glad consciousness that life had been given to her again. It was not a possession to be hoarded greedily, but a gift to be held in trust.

So the gift of God is eternal life. It is a gift of the Spirit, of "love, joy, peace, patience, kindness, goodness, faithfulness, gentleness, self-control," as Paul wrote to the Galatians (chapter 5). There is a temptation to think of this gift of the Spirit as given to special individuals, perhaps in some spectacular fashion. Scripturally, the gift is described as being for all Christians, as being given to the Church.

The gift of the Spirit is the power behind all our efforts as Christians. Without it we would be helpless. It is significant that the gifts described to the Galatians are all ones that must be exercised in a social context, in our dealings with others. Any sort of pride would destroy the effectiveness of such gifts as patience, kindness or any of the rest. Rather than prized possessions, tempting our human pride, they constitute a trust for which we are responsible.

Paradoxically, we cannot experience this new life until we know the meaning of death. Death is faced in the Scriptures as the cessation of physical life with the sorrow of separation and loss—a brutal fact of our existence. In the Old Testament it is sometimes indicated that we know death through evil. As in Proverbs: "In the path of righteousness is life, but the way of error leads to death" (Proverbs 12:28). The New Testament expands this connection and looks at death in three ways as related to human salvation.

Death is represented as the condition of the person apart from God, in rebellion against God. Paul wrote the Ephesians that alienated from God and his people they were "dead through the trespasses and sins." This is hardly in accord with the estimate we usually have of ourselves. To admit deadness contradicts a favorite human conceit—self-sufficiency. We like to think of ourselves as equal to our problems, able to overcome evil in our own strength. The gospel of success is entrenched in human thought and action. To be a "loser" is unthinkable. Life is best for "winners." To admit an emptiness or acknowledge a wrong is devastating. We are inclined to rationalize everything we do, find an excuse for every action. Yet the admission must be made if we are realistic about our condition. Death and evil go together. Self-indulgence, hate, greed, malice poison all of life. We are loath to admit our complicity in the evils which destroy our fellows; we refuse to picture ourselves in the role of oppressors, but a spiritual death, a dying of all that is decent and kind in us accompanies blindness to our failures. Life is seen in contrast to this condition as a gift of God's grace out of the riches of his mercy.

Death is seen in another way as being the *source* of life. Paul writes to the Romans:

> While we were yet helpless, at the right time Christ died for the
> ungodly. Why, one would hardly die for a righteous man–though
> perhaps for a good man one will even dare to die. But God shows
> his love for us in that while we were yet sinners Christ died for us.
> (Romans 5:6–8)

Christ's death was a revelation of the sacrificial love of God for us, a
love that has no limits, which makes possible a new life. No God
could save us except a suffering God, one who has shared our
human condition, who took the risk of being hated, despised, crucified for our sakes. It is impossible for us to imagine what it meant to
God to take such a step, to go so far. Perhaps the phrase in the
Apostles' Creed, "he descended into hell," gives an insight. The
memory of such infinite love is life-giving. It assures us that God
cares, that life is not meaningless and hopelessly bad. No matter
how evil the past has been, if God has shared this life with us, died
for us, then all is bearable, all pain can be transcended, all sin forgiven.

There is a third way of experiencing death, a corollary to
Christ's dying for us. Paradoxically, a renewed life depends on our
own dying. There is a dying to self, to the appetites and desires
which separate us from God, to the self-will that insists on having
its own way, to all that alienates us from our fellows and produces
hostility and fear. Such a dying does not mean simply the repression
of the feelings and desires which poison life, pushing such emotions
beneath the surface, away from conscious thought. It is a more radical process involving facing ourselves realistically minus all illu-
sions. It is an exposure that may be devastating, yet it clears the way
for the building of life upon a new foundation. Paul describes this
dying as being united to Christ in a cricifixion like his:

> We know that our old self was crucified with him so that the sinful
> body might be destroyed, and we might no longer be enslaved to
> sin. (Romans 6:6)

Can this be possible? A life is built around a self, its desires, needs
and values. Can all this die? Can life be so changed that self is no
longer the center of things? It can if we can identify with Christ in
his death.

It is not only to our appetites and passions that we die, but to all the self-justifying, self-saving attitudes and convictions, to a deadening and hopeless legalism. Paul wrote to the Galatians of his hopeless effort to find salvation through obedience to the law. He found in Christ deliverance from that struggle:

> For I through the law died to the law, that I might live to God. I have been crucified with Christ; it is no longer I who live, but Christ who lives in me; and the life I now live in the flesh I live by faith in the Son of God, who loved me and gave himself for me. (Galatians 2:19–20)

Carry this dying a step farther. We are called to follow in Christ's steps, deny ourselves, take up our crosses and follow him. The life we have through him is one that must be shared to be valid. If we have known a saving love in Christ, we share it by practicing a sacrificial love in our relationships with others. We cannot save another from drowning except by risking our own lives. We cannot care for the victims of an epidemic without the danger of becoming victims too. So we cannot share life without a certain dying, and the love we share is the most potent means of communicating the life we have known in Christ.

There is a death of pride required of us if we are to be effective instruments of Christ. I remember many years ago a man's telling me that I had failed him, had not met his spiritual needs. There is no doubt that every minister fails to meet the needs of some he tries to serve, but this man was a faithful friend and failure came close to home. It was a kind of death that destroyed complacency. It led to a reassessment of what I was trying to do, a new effort to let Christ work more effectively through me. Always we must yield ourselves to God as men who have passed out of death into life" (1 John 3:14).

T. S. Eliot in his poem, "Journey of the Magi," has one of these wise men remembering that journey after many years. It was a difficult one, costly in effort, often discouraging. He asks a question:

> . . . were we led all that way for
> Birth or Death? There was a Birth, certainly,
> We had evidence and no doubt. I had seen birth and death,
> But had thought they were different; this birth was

Hard and bitter agony for us, like Death, our death.
(T. S. Eliot, *Complete Poems and Plays*)

Such is the new birth in Christ. It finds its origin in his death, its consummation in ours. But at the end of the journey is life. The death of Christ for our sakes is not some distant event, unconnected with our present lives. Paul says in Romans 6:3 that Christians have been "baptized into his death." We share it, have a vital part in his sacrificial love as we are united with him. But the matter does not end here. Just as we are crucified with him, sharing his death, so we share his Resurrection. His conquest of death becomes our conquest as we identify with him. Death loses its power over us as we are set free from sin, freed from the fear of death. To Paul this transcendence of mortal life does not begin in some distant time. The Resurrection begins here and now as we "walk in newness of life."

We look at ourselves, perhaps after years of Christian experience, and we deplore our continued failures, our incompleteness, our lack of submission to Christ. Where is this promised new life made possible by Christ's death and Resurrection? Is it really ours? The answer is to be found in faith. Christ has made possible the life that can be through faith in him.

It does not matter what we have been. That can die. It does not matter who we are or how important we are in the eyes of the world. That perishes too. Being a celebrity or a nobody makes little difference. What really matters is that Christ take possession of us and live through us. I know of a woman who has had devastating experiences all her life. She grew up in a rough environment and had little education. She had marital mishaps, including a drunken husband who was a problem over the years. But somewhere along the way she found Christ as a reality in her experience and a singular faith has sustained her through troubles that would have soured and embittered most people. Through the years her letters have been accounts of battles won through faith in Christ. Her experience reminds us of Paul's statement " . . . we have this treasure in earthen vessels, to show that the transcendent power belongs to God and not to us" (2 Corinthians 4:7).

CHAPTER FOUR

Set Free to Live

The chapel at the prison farm had a past as an Army Quonset hut. The rounded metal structure had windows only at one end. At the other there was a large exhaust fan which labored valiantly to draw the hot, stifling air from the building. Unfortunately, it was too far from the platform where we sat to do much good. The pulpit was between the two windows and the air drawn in from each missed me entirely!

It was my turn to preach to the prisoners on a July Sunday afternoon. I had brought along a musician to play the battered piano and a young woman from our choir to sing. When the men were marched in from their quarters we did our best to have a worship service—using hymns they selected. I preached a sermon I hoped would be helpful. They were hot and we were hot, so we made it brief. Afterward we talked to a few who were willing to converse—a strained exercise. The men were taken back to their rooms and we drove back through a pleasant countryside in an airconditioned car to a world altogether different from theirs.

I felt a sense of frustration, as I usually do after talking to prisoners. There is a gap which separates those who have had their freedom taken from them and those of us who seemingly make our own choices about life. How to you reach people who live behind as many walls as these? They were prisoners not only of the state but also of the environment in which they had grown up, of bad habits, poor motivations, sheer desperation and despair.

Understanding is encouraged by the remembrance that we are

all prisoners of one kind or another. I am a prisoner of the culture in which I have been reared, of a standard of living I would be reluctant to abandon, of predjudices which seem to appear without my bidding, of bad habits, of the selfishness which keeps me from a true generosity, of fears that breed distrust of others. All of us can make a similar confession. Mutual understanding of our various bondages can be the first step toward the freedom which is a vital factor in our salvation.

Our bondage can be as varied as our styles of living. One would hardly think of this businessman as a captive, but there is evidence of it. On a certain morning he is late getting to his office because of heavy traffic. Tension mounts as he finds a list of telephone calls to make, more than he can manage before a morning conference. His wife calls to tell him of a P.T.A. meeting in the evening and a report he must make to the group. He remembers that he had promised to make some calls for the church. His children are expecting him to take them swimming in the late afternoon. Pressures! He wonders if he is free to make any choices for himself.

His wife has her own problems. The school P.T.A. is selling hot dogs to the kids today to obtain funds for the school library and she had been drafted to help. Her son is expecting her to come to the baseball game today to see him play. Her daughter needs to be taken to her dancing class. She must find time to prepare a devotional for her church circle. She is on a committee to plan an entertainment at the country club and must find some time for that. Her husband has expectations of her too. Is freedom possible for either husband or wife in the midst of pressures and demands which often conflict?

Their children feel hemmed in too. They are subject to rules made by home, school, community and society in general. There are peer groups which insist on conformity in dress, conduct, tastes in music or entertainment. It may be the in-thing to smoke a joint or do something else forbidden. If they do not conform they are simply out of it. Sometimes the expectations of society, the community, the church seem to be too much to bear and children become rebellious. They long for situations where there is no one around to tell them what to do, how to behave. Freedom, as they see it, seems far away.

Add to this some other confining factors. Most of us find some real limitations in our finances. A pastor was counseling some young marrieds and found that many of them had no idea how much they owed. They were barely able to keep up with the interest payments on their credit cards! We may be prisoners of the loan companies. If we are poor the bondage is worse. People in poverty are sometimes at the mercy of capricious officials and are living in degrading subservience. If we live under a dictatorial regime freedom may be a myth. Some may find themselves in prison if they differ with those in power. We can grow so used to political bondage that we feel secure in it, probably with little reason. In many places such factors as race or sex may bring severe restrictions.

The plight of one of the high schools in our city has been publicized lately. It is an all-black vocational high school. Scores on literacy tests have been distressingly low with keen embarrassment for the young people involved. The order necessary for learning is lacking. The morale of both the teachers and the pupils has reached a low ebb. There is bitterness and rebellion on the part of both. These young people are really prisoners of a system in which segregation is still a powerful factor. Poverty and poor education over a long period have created a prison from which it will be difficult to escape.

We can be imprisoned by our mistakes and the unwillingness of society to forgive and forget them. A person who has been a criminal and in prison is a prisoner of the past. When he leaves prison, regardless of changes in his attitudes and motivations, he finds it difficult to find a place in society. Doors to employment and a place of respect in the community are closed. Unless he has help he might as well be in prison still. Freedom may be denied in so many other ways.

Internally we suffer from bondages of a different kind, deadly addictions, appetites and desires that destroy, malignant hates and fears. We may be in bondage to customs of our communities which keep us from being open and generous in our treatment of all people. My enslavement may be to an image of myself that I have created, a conception of my role in life, an exaggerated belief in my own importance. If a person is a celebrity he must conform to the image he has created for the public.

A minister has found wide recognition and popularity. Crowds hear him and respond to his messages. He associates with well-known people in many occupations. He is quoted widely and makes pronouncements on many subjects. In time he finds that he is a prisoner of a popular conception of his character and powers. How difficult to find freedom from such a prison.

A politician of power and influence holds tightly to an authority which is threatened from many quarters. In the passage of time he has mellowed somewhat and seems to be seeking peace for his country, but he is a prisoner of his past. There was a time when he was a man of violence, using any measures at hand to defeat his enemies. He is still subject to the passions and motivations of the past. Can he ever be free to build peace?

Bondage may assume many forms. Our desires to be comfortable, to be powerful, to be popular may be quite sufficient to enslave. In many ways we are slaves to ourselves and this slavery may be more powerful than external restraints placed upon us. The total life of persons and the society of which they are a part is vitally affected by such subjection.

There is a longing for freedom which may be covered up or disguised but never completely stifled. The morning paper recently had several evidences of this insistent desire. A leading article discussed the proposed rules to control spy agencies which infringe on the privacy of citizens. The current insistence on human rights was discussed in an editorial. Another editorial writer spoke of America as "the sentinel of freedom." This was not too happy a choice of words for freedom can scarcely be forced on other nations. Evidences of the need for freedom are everywhere, from the violence-maintained countries like Uganda and Paraguay to the suburban home with its claims and pressures. Basically our longing for freedom is a part of being human. It is a fundamental passion which has preoccupied humanity for centuries. Currently it manifests itself in challenges to bondages which many thought could not be changed.

There are several reactions to this human longing for freedom and the changes it brings. We say it is the fundamental right of every person to be free. Our nation was founded on the idea. We proclaim our belief in human rights. We celebrate the achievement of national freedom on the Fourth of July each year. We have great admiration for individualists who insist on their freedom—if they do not trouble us too much!

On the other hand we have a great fear of freedom. We can easily cite its misuses and abuses. Challenges to authority frighten us even when the protest is seemingly justified. We are understandably suspicious of a freedom which means nothing more than having our own way or doing as we please, regardless of the effect on others. License is an abuse of freedom. It is like the action of a car without brakes on a downhill slope. Obstinacy is an abuse of freedom—the action of an individual or group making unyielding demands, unwilling to negotiate a settlement of difficulties. If freedom is defined simply as "the ability to act independently," or "detached," "unconditional," "unobstructed," it can just as well be a danger as a source of life. In the days of the judges in ancient Israel it was said that "everyone did what was right in his own eyes." The result was moral chaos. Libertinism, which recognizes no restraints or responsibilities, can produce the same effect at any time.

Security as well as freedom is needed. Some elderly people in our city have the choice of living in an apartment house which is so protected that they have practically no contacts with younger families or in a neighborhood where they can have fellowship with young families only at the price of being subject to attacks. Freedom can be denied either way. The situation points to the need for a better solution than either of these options. We are concerned not only about being free, but about being secure. We endeavor to strike a precarious balance between the two. Security sometimes seems to have the stronger appeal. Some of us would rather be safe, even if it involves a certain rigidity in society.

All this suggests a question. Is freedom essentially good, or is it a tool by which goodness may come? Is it a factor in salvation? Paul wrote a letter to Philemon, a member of the church at Colossae, concerning Onesimus, a runaway slave he had persuaded to return to his master. He wanted Philemon to treat this man as a brother rather than a slave, but he says, "I preferred to do nothing without your consent in order that your goodness might not be by compulsion but of your own free will." (verse 14) Their freedom to do good of their own choice evidently brought freedom in time to another human being.

Paul came to this conviction about the need of freedom through a long struggle. Reared in a strict legalistic tradition, he had an ingrained conviction that obedience to the law would save, make goodness possible. In his letter to the Galatians he described the law as a "school teacher" to lead toward salvation, but he came to the conclusion from personal experience that faith alone could save. He could serve God only in freedom, led by the Spirit. He wrote, "For freedom Christ has set us free." (Gal. 5:1) There is always the temptation, which Paul had for so long, to think that the good life is based essentially on the strict enforcement of rules. We can understand that. We insist that authorities be strict. The constraint of laws can bring a guidance and protection which is sorely needed, but it can never make people good. In fact too much reliance on enforced conduct, together with a certain pride in our own obedience, can make us so self-righteous that it is difficult for others to live with us. Love and trust can never be compelled. I did not learn to love and trust my parents through any requirement that I do so, only through the love and trust they demonstrated toward me. God never compels us to love him. It must be voluntary.

So freedom is a prerequisite of goodness, instrumental in our salvation. It is manifested in human longings under many circumstances, born of a conviction that life is crippled and unfulfilled if human beings are subject to any sort of slavery. Some would draw a line between this universal need of freedom and the freedom we need as Christians, freedom from all that separates us from God, freedom from the condemnation of God through the gracious sacrifice of Christ. Can such a line be drawn? It is doubtful if it can, for in all human bondage there is implicit the denial of the love which is at the heart of Christian freedom. The human longing for freedom and the desperate need for liberation have an answer in the purpose of God to save us.

God has been liberating his people for a long time. One of the oldest memories of the Hebrew people, repeated over and over in their writings, was of their deliverance from Egypt. The Israelites were enslaved by a king of Egypt who did not know their powerful ancestor, Joseph. They cried to God for help and he provided a deliverer in Moses, who managed to bring them out of Egypt and through the Red Sea, freeing them from bondage. The Hebrews found in this liberation the birth of their nation.

As God had liberated them, so they felt there was an obligation to liberate others. This is seen in their laws in Exodus 21 and Deuteronomy 15, which show their struggle with the problem of human slavery and their feeling of obligation to mitigate its evil effects. The concern shown in their laws for the care of such repressed groups as the poor, the aliens and illegitimate children shows a sense of obligation to the less fortunate, growing out of gratitude for their own liberation. The prophet Jeremiah reproached King Zedikiah for his enslavement of his people, denouncing him for breaking the covenant which God had made with the nation when he brought them out of Egypt, an agreement violated by taking away his people's freedom. God's will for his people was freedom.

The bondage of evil was a frequent theme in the writings of the prophets of Israel. "The iniquities of the wicked ensnare him, and he is caught in the toils of his sin," writes the author of Proverbs (5:22). In Isaiah 59 God is pictured as both saving and condemning:

> Behold, the LORD's hand is not shortened, that it cannot save,
> or his ear dull that it cannot hear;
> but your iniquities have made a separation
> between you and your God,
> and your sins have hid his face from you
> so that he does not hear. (Isaiah 59:1–2)

Then follows a most graphic description of the sins which separate people from God—murder, lies, dishonesty, violence, injustice. The prisons which such evils construct are described—moral blindness, despair, denial of God, oppression. God is pictured as a Redeemer who comes to turn men from their wrong.

The vision of the Old Testament is of a God who frees human beings from every bondage. There is a triumphant expression of this faith in Isaiah 61:1:

> The Spirit of the Lord GOD is upon me,
> because the LORD has anointed me

> to bring good tidings to the afflicted;
> he has sent me to bind up the brokenhearted,
> to proclaim liberty to the captives,
> and the opening of the prison to those who are bound. . . .

At the very beginning of his ministry Christ stated the purpose of his mission in the world in terms of liberation by reading in the synagogue in Nazareth this same passage from Isaiah. The translation he read has some differences, but the message is the same. Our Lord's work was to be a fulfillment of the ancient prophet's words, "good news to the poor," "release to the captives," "recovering of sight to the blind," liberty for the oppressed. These words speak to the condition of all people in bondage. In Luke's version of the beatitudes (6:20–30) the same feeling for the poor, the enslaved, the sick and the oppressed is expressed. In Luke 14 Christ praises the humble and asks that the poor, maimed, unfortunate folk be brought to a feast. The "losers" of the world, the outcasts of society, received his chief consideration. He made friends with prostitutes and publicans, captives in different ways not only of their own lust and greed, but also of the binding situations in society in which they found themselves. In the home of Simon the Pharisee (Luke 7:36ff.) he offered freedom through forgiveness not only to the respectable householder but also to the woman of the streets who washed his feet and anointed them with precious ointment.

Christ came to free men from every captivity, from the bondage of the closed mind and the slavery of sin:

> Jesus then said to the Jews who had believed in him, "If you continue in my word, you are truly my disciples, and you will know the truth, and the truth will make you free." They answered him, "We are descendants of Abraham, and have never been in bondage to any one. How is it that you say, 'You will be made free'?"

> Jesus answered them, "Truly, truly, I say to you, every one who commits sin is a slave to sin. The slave does not continue in the house for ever; the son continues for ever. So if the Son makes you free, you will be free indeed." (John 8:31–36)

The liberating power of Jesus was the force that made new men of his followers. They were freed from fear after his Resurrection.

They proclaimed boldly a message that was unacceptable to those in power. They risked prison to obey God rather than men. They found a new freedom from sin. Paul wrote of those who "having been set free from sin have become slaves of righteousness." (Romans 6:18). Freed from bondage to evil they became willing servants of what was right and good. Paul described their previous experience as a bondage to the "flesh." He was not speaking of the "flesh" in terms of our physical life or human nature in general but rather in terms of our nature as perverted by sin and enslaved to self-interest, including the indulgence of all our greedy and hateful passions, a life in opposition to God. "For the mind that is set on the flesh," he says, "is hostile to God; it does not submit to God's law, indeed it cannot; and those who are in the flesh cannot please God" (Romans 8:7–8). He described a new freedom of those who live "according to the Spirit," "those who set their minds on the things of the Spirit." He is describing a life with a new center and a new direction. It was not a life of escape from the world and its problems, but rather a freedom to live purposefully and lovingly in the midst of pressures and restraints. Self-discipline is necessary for such a life. The first letter of Peter gives this instruction: "Live as free men, yet without using your freedom as a pretext for evil; but live as servants of God" (1 Peter 2:16). It is not a life of irresponsibility, of license to do as you please, but rather a life with a new allegiance, a new set of responsibilities, with a freedom to love and obey God.

Many varieties of human bondage have been described. All of us are captives in some fashion. Each has his own particular slavery or slaveries growing out of the circumstances of his life. Each of us reacts in a different way—rebellion, submission, or some kind of accommodation. Each of us needs help, liberation. It is this universal human plight to which the gospel addresses itself. The work of liberation must touch all of life, the totality of human existence. If any area of life is untouched there is loss. There is no way of compartmentalizing our existence.

Our various bondages have much in common. Each in some way degrades human beings. The enslaved person is deprived of his dignity as a child of God. Whether we are slaves of poverty, political domination, social discrimination, an evil past, sinful passions, dope or whatever, we are made less than what God intended us to be. If we enslave others in some fashion both the person dominating and the one in subjection are diminished. Our faith has an answer to this problem. Paul wrote to the Galatians that when we are in Christ "There is neither Jew nor Greek, there is neither slave nor free, there is neither male nor female: for you are all one in Christ Jesus" (Galatians 3:28). When we are in Christ we can no longer say or feel that people of another race, another class or another sex are inferior. In Christ we are all the same. The freedom revolution that this idea of equality before God started is still being worked out in the world. It is a reality wherever we are freed by Christ from the enslaving notions of superiority or inferiority, as Christ helps us to lay aside our prejudices.

All types of bondages are destructive of relationships with God and with our fellows. The bondage of sin keeps us from communion with God. When something takes the place of God in our lives, even important things like family or business, work or pleasure, then our freedom in God's world is diminished. There is an important connection between worship and freedom, going beyond the question of whether churches are left open. When God is not worshiped or his work is neglected a different set of motivations and ideals takes over. There is a change in the total life of society. Freedom is endangered.

Similarly, God is rejected as we acquiesce in any kind of human bondage. Estrangement comes as we endeavor to dominate other human beings. There can be no trust, no truly loving service in such a relationship. People under such an arrangement may be held together by common interests, but there is no real understanding. The teachers who have meant most to me in my own education have been not the authoritative figures but those who invited me to a common search for truth. Whenever there is economic or political bondage there is a smoldering resentment under the surface on one side and a fear of rebellion on the other which creates an atmosphere of violence. Freedom comes as Christ brings us together in a common concern for each other's needs.

Our own liberation is fulfilled as we liberate others. Our freedom in Christ is not a private reality to be cherished and made secure. It involves others. Peace, love and justice go beyond the individual person to the society of which he is a part. Freedom is very much a social reality. Society cannot be renewed without it. We become a part of God's universal saving process as we help others to be free. How can this be done?

We liberate others as we become sensitive to their needs. This may come through listening to them. A pastor tells of visiting an estranged member and "listening to his pain." To restore openness may be the first step in liberation. If people can learn to talk to each other, to understand each other's feelings and problems in the spirit of Christ, freedom may come.

Liberation may involve assuming responsibility for others in their plight. Freedom makes it possible for us to bear one another's burdens even when this is unpopular and provokes criticism. A young pastor of an influential church is moved by the sad condition of the people of a slum area who are protesting against the poor condition of their houses and the insensitivity of those who own them and will not keep them in repair. Liberation may mean joining them in their protest regardless of the consequences. We need the freedom that Christ gives in order to lose our lives that we may gain them.

Freedom comes with detachment, when we lose sight of ourselves and give our strength and effort to a larger goal, the service of God and the needs of our fellows. Paul gave us insight into this when he wrote to the Philippians, " . . . forgetting what lies behind and straining forward to what lies ahead, I press on toward the goal for the prize of the upward call of God in Christ Jesus" (Philippians 3:13-14). Yet in our striving we come to the realization that freedom is a gift, that it comes from being mastered by something larger than ourselves.

When we know the love of Christ and can forget ourselves through that love there comes a liberation from all the forces that enslave us. We can rise above them in his strength, above the pressures of work and society, above the tyranny of customs and rules, above the dark passions that bind us. We can rise above them in his strength. Life is futile unless we can devote it to something infinitely important. So we want to be mastered in order that we may really be free. Paul wrote to the Corinthians, "... all things are yours ... and you are Christ's and Christ is God's" (1 Corinthians 3:21, 23). Life is unlimited if it belongs to Christ. He sets us free to live.

CHAPTER FIVE

The Miracle of Growth

Shortly before leaving the pastorate of a city church I had lunch with an old friend. He told me of what had meant most to him in his Christian experience in the years he had been an officer in our church—a growth in Christian stewardship. I had seen that growth and rejoiced in it. His interest in the work had grown wider. He had become sensitive to need. His dedication had deepened. He had enabled the church to take many forward steps and in addition had helped the various denominations to work together. I was glad that he felt that he was growing, that his life was developing through a sense of responsibility which found its source in God's love for him. Christians may grow in many ways, each according to his own nature and gifts.

There are many ideas of growth. I thought of how this man's conception contrasted with the usual notion of growth in our city. We seemed to be fascinated in differing degrees by size. It was a growing city, constantly extending its borders, and is now one of the largest in the nation. Manufacturing companies, business enterprises, law firms, institutions and churches seemed to be rated by how big they were. But bigness is not always goodness. People may grow in worldly importance, social prestige, political status, wealth or power and yet fail to grow spiritually. We live in a success-oriented world in which achievement has very definite measurements in the public mind. Sometimes growth of a less tangible variety is underrated and neglected.

Jesus was most interested in growth, in the individuals he

touched, in the kingdom he came to establish. We are told that he grew in "wisdom and in stature, and in favor with God and man" (Luke 2:52). When all the implications of these categories are considered, it is difficult to think of a better description of human growth. He was eager that his disciples should grow and encouraged them in many ways. He challenged them with parables of development—about the tiny mustard seed that grew into a great tree, the grain sown in a field that produced a rich harvest. He used the parables of the talents and the pounds to speak of the growth of people in faithfulness. As he trained his followers he never allowed them to become complacent. He challenged their prejudices about other races, the Samaritans for instance; about religious practices which no longer had meaning; about customs that kept them in bondage and about their contempt for social failures. He supplied the dynamics for growth. John writes of Christ's followers, "to all who received him, who believed in his name, he gave power to become children of God" (John 1:12). Christ spent most of his brief ministry training his disciples, helping them to grow. Through his inspiration they grew from frightened persons, uncertain and undependable, to the faithful group that made possible the Christian church.

The earliest writers of the church looked on salvation as a growing relationship with God and their fellows. Paul wrote to the Corinthians, "For the word of the cross is folly to those who are perishing, but to us who are *being saved* it is the power of God" (1 Corinthians 1:18). In 2 Corinthians 2:15 he writes again of those who are *"being saved."* Life in Christ was a continuing process, never static. In the letter to the Ephesians, he speaks of leaving behind a childishness in which we are easily led astray.

> Rather, speaking the truth in love we are to grow up in every way into him who is the head, into Christ. (Ephesians 4:15)

It is a process which goes beyond following an example or obeying a command. Growth comes as we are "strengthened with might through his Spirit in the inner man," as Christ dwells in our hearts through faith, as we are rooted and grounded in love, as we know the love of Christ and are "filled with all the fulness of God" (Ephesians 3:16–19). It is a growth made possible through God's indwelling and its goal is "mature manhood," "the measure of the stature of the fulness of Christ" (Ephesians 4:13). Peter expresses his hope that his correspondents may "grow up to salvation" (1 Peter 2:2). In his second letter he instructs them to "grow in the grace and knowledge of our Lord and Savior Jesus Christ" (2 Peter 3:18).

Knowledge has often been the measure of Christian growth. Paul thought it valuable. He wrote in 1 Corinthians 13:12b, "Now I know in part; then I shall understand fully, even as I have been fully understood." The world measures personal growth to a great extent in terms of accumulated knowledge and skill. They are essential. If we reach adulthood without a certain basic fund of knowledge and skills, life is crippled as a result. We value knowledge in the Christian life. We need to know the facts about our faith, what the Bible teaches, our great heritage of religious knowledge which grows out of centuries of Christian experience and thought. Without such knowledge we are vague and uncertain, unable to give a reason for our faith or to understand its meaning for our lives.

What is most important is the use we make of knowledge. It has been used to create violent means of destruction, dangerous both to humanity and the environment. It can be used to manipulate people and increase the power and prestige of those who have it. It can be the source of vanity and pride. It has a way of getting beyond us. The knowledge explosion, the vast accumulation of facts beyond our ability to grasp, has created problems despite the use of computers, which have their own problems.

On the other hand, knowledge has made possible the kind of life we have today, improved in many ways through medicine, technology, better methods of producing food, etc. Life is richer in spite of the obvious losses and dangers.

Our great need is for wisdom, which can mean the ability to use our accumulated knowledge for the best ends. Our difficulty is that both wisdom and knowledge are limited. God's wisdom, his "unsearchable judgments" (Romans 11:33) are contrasted with man's wisdom, which is never complete. Yet we are challenged to develop

in wisdom and to demonstrate our growth through our deeds. James
in his letter asks:

> Who is wise and understanding among you? By his good life let
> him show his works in the meekness of wisdom. (James 3:13)

We need to grow in wisdom, in the right application of knowledge. It means the development of sound judgment, of the ability to
judge what is right and wrong. If our children are growing in wisdom we need not worry if all sides of every matter in dispute are
presented to them. Wisdom may grow in many ways as our experience broadens and we have more background for our decisions. It
grows with our ability to search after truth, to maintain open minds,
to face reality with honesty. It grows as we see ourselves clearly, delivered through the grace of God from self-deception. Wisdom
comes as we learn to take and use criticism and as we learn from
our mistakes. It comes in dialogue as we learn from those we meet.
Most of our learning is in meeting. Above all wisdom is a gift of
God, learned from him as we face all the situations of life in his
strength.

The goal of our growth, as Paul described it in Ephesians, is
"mature manhood," "the measure of the stature of the fulness of
Christ." Maturity goes beyond knowledge, in some ways beyond
wisdom. It involves the total person, all his emotional reactions.
Jesus told a story about children playing games in the marketplace.
Some refused to play because others would not play the games they
wanted to play. He was criticizing the immaturity of the critics of
John the Baptist and himself. Nothing they said or did could please
the critics (Matthew 11:16–19). The immature person demands that
he be satisfied regardless of all other circumstances. A popular song
speaks of "grown-up children." None of us can escape that description entirely. There are times when our emotions get the best of us
and we act like children. Somehow growth has not taken place. In
another fashion we may be so hardened in a certain mold that
growth is impossible. Mature personhood may seem to be beyond
us. We may want maturity but not be able to face its demands. The
old self has to die and that we cannot face.

Maturity finds its fulfillment in love. This is the great insight of the gospel. Paul speaks in Ephesians of "being rooted and grounded in love" (3:17) and of knowing "the love of Christ which surpasses knowledge" (3:19). This is the basis of maturity. He says that it is through "speaking the truth in love, we are to grow up in every way into him who is the head, into Christ" (4:15). This verse has vast implications for all human relationships. Paul is saying that growth comes for us as all human communications are carried on in the spirit of love. In our attempts to bring settlements of disputes, is our motivation the welfare of all concerned? Do we communicate this concern? If truth and love can be combined in our dealings with other human beings, there is hope for peace, for a more enduring fellowship among all men. It is significant that Paul ended his great poem on love, 1 Corinthians 13, with a thought on growth. "When I was a child, I spoke like a child, I thought like a child, I reasoned like a child; when I became a man I gave up childish ways."

Growing in love means more than an increase in affection. This kind of love may degenerate into a possessiveness which forbids growth for all parties involved. When we attempt to make all decisions for those we love we keep them from the development which comes only through responsible choice. "Smother love" takes over. The independence of spirit so needed is denied. Nor is love realized in indulgence. In a recent TV play a young man was in trouble over smuggling narcotics. His father could not understand it. He and his wife had always given him everything he desired. But satisfying every whim did not mean growth in love for either parents or child. Growth in love means the development of understanding, sensitivity to the feelings and needs of others, identification with others in their joys and sorrows. To grow means to see and treat people as "whobodies" rather than "anybodies" as Charles and Ann Morse so aptly describe them in *Whobody There*. It is to see the person in every human being.

We grow as we become concerned about the other fellow. Conversely, people tend to grow as others become concerned about them. A novel by a young black writer, Frankcina Glass, entitled *Marvin and Tige* is a sensitive story of a young black boy reared in a slum where crime and prostitution thrive. He steals in order to eat. He is illiterate and his language is deplorable. His mother dies and in despair he tries to take his life. He is kept from it when he meets a kindly white man who has his own problems of loneliness and disillusionment. The man shelters the boy, offers him friendship and loving care; and the boy begins to change in his language, actions, attitudes. Firmness, honesty and compassion brought about the change. The man develops a new interest in life as his love for the boy grows. Eventually the boy finds a place for himself in a family of his own race, but he returns to assure the man of his gratitude and continuing love. It is a simple story but one with profound meaning for human growth.

Growth is an individual matter. None of us grows in the same way. Each has his own point of departure. Dr. Richard C. Cabot in his book *The Art of Ministering to the Sick* gave an illustration from a medical experiment which gives insight. It was discovered that a bit of muscle or other bodily tissue could survive and grow apart from the body in a solution in which it was fed. The tissue put out a new column of cells and grew appreciably. There was a growing edge. The same thing happens to the live oak trees in my yard. In the spring they shed the leaves which have been held all winter because the new leaves are coming on—a growing edge in the life of the tree. Dr. Cabot suggested that every person has a growing edge where real personal growth begins. Sometimes we are tempted to give up on ourselves and others. Nothing seems to be developing. We seem to be at a standstill. But there is something in each of us that transcends our present condition, some undeveloped possibility which God has given. God is always challenging us to break through the shell and create something new. The growing edge in a person's life is the place where he has an interest, where something creative is aroused in him. It is a place not only where a need is felt and where a hunger needs satisfaction, but also where an opportunity is given for participation. It may require the trust of others, a belief they have in our potentialities. We support each other in this matter. Regardless of the circumstances it is always a miracle when it happens, a work of God's grace.

The unexpectedness of growth in human life is amazing. Some years ago the church I served saw the need for a program of recreation for neighborhood children in the area around us. Delinquency

was rife. The children had no play facilities. The church worked together with the Y.M.C.A. and the merchants of the neighborhood to
establish a Friday afternoon program of games, crafts, stories and
refreshments. Juvenile delinquency became almost nonexistent. We
asked for volunteers to carry on the work and had a response beyond our hopes. One of the women serving had never engaged in
work of this kind before to my knowledge. She developed skills and
interest which eventually made her the leader in the enterprise. Who
would have thought that a dozen years later she would be still working at it? The program continued until the neighborhood changed
and the nearby school was discontinued, and she was with it to the
end.

Opportunities for growth come when there are creative contacts
between people who are not brought together normally. The church
I serve has a month-long summer program for black children with
training in various skills combined with worship, recreation and
good food. I doubt if we teach them very much in knowledge and
skills. The time is too short. They have learned something about
working with wood, making gardens, cooking, sewing, art, etc.; but
the chief value comes in the fact that forty or so church members
work with sixty children. There is growth in understanding, appreci-
ation of each other, interest in each other's lives. It is a memorable
experience. Cynthia, one of the young people who attended, came
to see us recently. She is a forlorn small girl of sixteen who hardly
looks fourteen. We asked if she were in school and found that she
was not. She had to look after her baby! We felt helpless to do anything for her. The important thing was that in her loneliness she had
returned to a place where she had known love and interest. Something had happened in the fellowship she had known with us.

A time of crisis may also be a time of growth. A woman came to
me with a question I could not answer, "Why did my husband have
to die?" I could have replied with the standard answers, that death
is the natural end for human beings, that we have to trust in God,
accept what comes in faith. She needed more, the opportunity to explore the significance of the life she had shared with another person,
the meaning of this change for her life ahead, the hope of another

life, reunion. In the process of exploring these questions she probably never found a complete answer to the original one, but she grew as she came to a new understanding of herself and her faith. As people face the crises of loss of a family member, failure, illness or any other shattering experience there is always the possibility of developing new resources, becoming stronger and more mature in every way. Their growth is a response in faith to a time of testing.

The choices we make, particularly the ones which affect the direction life takes, provide opportunities for growth. The businessman mentioned in the first chapter of this book had to make a choice between the security of an established career in manufacturing and the insecurity of an elected office. As he took the step of running for that office and giving up his business he grew in sympathy with the people who had known discrimination and in willingness to take the risks involved in meeting their needs. We grow as we choose the ways in which we shall invest our lives. Our conception of what is worthwhile, our entire set of values, may grow in the process.

Challenge enters into the process of growth. We cease to grow when there is nothing ahead that we can attempt. It is sad to talk to people who feel that life is over so far as any accomplishment on their part is concerned. It is inspiring to find an elderly woman who has been ill anxious to get back to her volunteer work in the church kitchen. There is still something for her to do. A famous author was being interviewed on "Book Beat" on TV and was asked what was his best book. The answer was obvious—his next one. He said he had always wanted to write a fine book. An avid tennis player always wants a strong opponent. A lawyer is challenged to do his best by the toughest adversary. The surgeon exercises his greatest skill in the most difficult operation. There is no greater challenge than a truly Christian life. Paul issued such a challenge to the Colossians:

> If then you have been raised with Christ, seek the things that are above, where Christ is, seated at the right hand of God. Set your minds on things that are above, not on things on earth. (Colossians 3:1–2)

The supreme challenge is to identify with Christ, to be able to say, with Paul, "For to me to live is Christ, and to die is gain" (Philippians 1:21) or "It is no longer I who live but Christ who lives in me" (Galatians 2:20). We can never be what Christ might be in any situation or do what he might have done. But the challenge is for us to so forget ourselves that Christ takes over and makes us his instruments in the world. Then we shall "grow up in every way into him who is the head" (Ephesians 4:15). It is a growth that never ceases, which can never be brought to completion.

Growth is never confined to the individual. It is a community process as well. Others are always affected. Paul describes it as culminating in the growth of the community of believers, the church. The fellowship of believers is the soil in which the individual Christian's growth takes place, but there is group development as well. The growth of the individual member of the church is crucial for the growth of the church. Our growth as individuals determines in great measure the development of our society. The growing Christian is the truly living Christian, affecting the whole world.

CHAPTER SIX

The Possibility of Change

It happens so often. He comes home tense and irritated from the office. Something is said that starts a quarrel. He strikes her and a fight begins. She ends up battered but is ashamed to call the police. The love they had for each other is being destroyed. There must be a change. Is it possible?

Jane has been having trouble with her drinking. If she takes one cocktail she must have another, and soon she becomes maudlin and unable to control herself. When she is sober afterward she resolves that it will never happen again, but it does. Can this pattern be changed before she becomes a derelict?

There is an area in our city near an old abandoned railroad station that has become almost uninhabitable. Buildings are boarded up. Warehouses are crumbling. Rot, rust and weeds are taking over. Human life is being corrupted. It is dangerous to go there after dark. Even in the daytime the merchants often will open their doors only when the customer identifies himself. Close to the heart of the city, what is now a slum could be an asset to the community, but change must come. Is it possible?

Changes are needed everywhere. We would like to change, to be free of those things that make life unbearable. Sometimes it seems easier to change the inner city than it does to change the inner man!

Change is both comforting and disturbing to us. We are just as uneasy about change as we are about freedom. On all sorts of levels and in many contexts we both desire and fear it. We want something new as long as it is attractive, innovative, exciting. Novelty is appealing. We like change when it brings freedom from something that is disturbing. But when change means giving up habits, routines, values and goals or when it involves conflict or sacrifice, then we are reluctant to accept it.

Change can be good, bad or indifferent. When the houses of an older, charming section of a city are destroyed to make room for the gray efficiency of urban "progress" there may be irreparable loss. When swamps are drained and a bird and animal refuge is destroyed to make room for another apartment section, something valuable may be lost. There are other changes which make life more abundant by removing filthy living conditions, all the ugliness that degrades human life. There is change in the crumbling of an individual's character just as there is change when a new beginning is made and life is reconstructed. Like freedom, change is merely an instrument to be used for good or evil.

No matter what our sentiments are about change it is undeniable that more has happened in our century to make the world and its inhabitants different than ever before in human history. Technological and industrial changes have revolutionized the lives of the majority of mankind. Changes in medicine and all health care have lengthened the lives of many. Political changes have made old maps obsolete and brought into being new kinds of societies. The rate of change has been so rapid that people are bewildered, confused by the new world in which they live. Accommodation is difficult. We rejoice in benefits while longing for simpler days. Our values have not kept pace with the changes undergone. We find it difficult to keep up morally with the changes that have occurred in society and its customs. The relation of faith to life is obscured. The really important question is not whether there shall be change, but the direction of change and the goals sought.

Christianity is intimately concerned with change. Salvation means change for those who experience it. Jesus was well aware of the conflict between the old and the new in all of life and its relevance to the new life he promised to all who followed him. Several of his short parables deal with the subject: the new patch on an old garment, the new wine in old wineskins, the householder who brought out of his treasures what was new and old. It was no wonder that he upset the Pharisees, the guardians of the accepted order of the time. He was frankly an innovator. His coming was to be like a wedding, a joyful occasion which celebrated a new relationship, not like the burdened and desolate past with its long prayers and legal rigor. No one sewed new cloth on a threadbare garment. Any housewife would know that it would tear away again. No one placed new wine in old, cracked leather wineskins that could not stand the pressure. The new wine of the gospel had to come in new forms. Prejudice and legalism had to give way before the doors were opened to reach out to all the world with a transforming message of salvation. Christ knew that there was treasure in the old so long as it did not make the new impossible or impotent, but he insisted that change must come both in individuals and in the world. He was following in the steps of prophets like Amos and Jeremiah who had insisted on change and renewal.

Jesus made it plain that the new way of life he brought would bring change in human beings. He startled Nicodemus by saying that the change needed in his life was so great that to experience it would be like being born again, the strongest way possible of expressing it. The new life through the Spirit's work in a person's heart was made possible through God's sending his own Son into the world to demonstrate the love of God for the world. It was so different from what Nicodemus had known that it would require a complete change in him. Old attitudes and values would have to change as well as evil practices be forsaken. Christ made such a change in the lives of those he touched. Change still comes as men know him. Paul described it as an ongoing process, continually taking place:

> Now the Lord is the Spirit, and where the Spirit of the Lord is there is freedom. And we all, with unveiled face, beholding the glory of the Lord, are being changed into his likeness from one degree of glory to another; for this comes from the Lord who is the Spirit. (2 Corinthians 3:17–18)

The need for change is evident in the scriptural descriptions of the human condition. To emphasize the power of God to save those who have faith in Christ Paul in Romans 1 describes human wickedness in vivid terms. Idolatry, sexual immorality, envy, murder, strife, deceit, malignity, gossip, slander and many other evils are condemned. It is a gloomy picture of a world that needed change. Is our own so different? Wickedness is still with us. Evil is just as deadly as ever. There is hope in the fact that we sometimes recognize its nature without self-deceit. I once wrote a paper on the evils condemned by the church in the last century and the early years of this one. Such things as drunkenness, gambling, sabbath-breaking, sexual misconduct and other personal sins were condemned; but nothing was said of war, poverty, oppression, racial discrimination, corruption in public office and other evils whose presence points to the need for drastic change. The need for individual change is still with us and is seen with deeper discernment as we understand more fully our unfaithfulness to God and the damage we do to our fellows. We need to see also the changes which must come in the world.

Karl Menninger in his book *Whatever Became of Sin?* eloquently describes the evils we face. Speaking of human beings, he says:

> Many of them live lives of great comfort and ease while thousands die of starvation daily. Millions, barely surviving, exist most miserably, working at monotonous drudgery. Conscripts are coerced to hurl fire, poisons, and explosives at "enemies" whom they resemble but do not know, and have only fictitious reasons for fearing or hating. Those not at war engage in angry dissensions over property, priorities, privilege, policy, and popularity. Fear and uncertainty, even among the prosperous, lead many citizens to rearm themselves with privately owned killing machines as in earlier days (but more deadly weapons). (page 5)

Is it possible that we do not grasp the depth of change that is necessary? In some ways tremendous strides have been made. New ways of feeding and healing people have been developed. A host of people have given themselves to the task of meeting desperate human need. There is a determination to avoid nuclear war which would destroy us all, although violence still plagues us. But sometimes it seems we are more interested in changes in the design of our cars or gadgets than in our ability to care for vital human needs. Change is sought on a trivial level. Our transgressions, according to the television advertisements which capture our attention, are foul breath, underarm odor, gray wash, a sour stomach, etc. Change can come through the proper brands of mouthwash, deodorants, detergents, digestive pills and like remedies. The changes produced will create happy, robust, sexually attractive people. It is a problem of attention and of the realization that change that matters grows out of sacrificial love, not out of our self-serving desires.

Change has many obstacles. In Samuel Beckett's play *Happy Days*, both characters sit mired in sand up to their waists at the beginning. As the play goes on they are more deeply buried. At the end only their heads stick out. This is symbolic of the difficulty of change in the world in which we live. A relentless culture binds us to established patterns. Peer groups impose their own variety of restriction on change. The so-called "liberated" may be far from it, having chosen their own prisons.

Resistance to change may grow out of complacency. Many have difficulty with the bugler who sounds reveille when they want to continue their slumbers. Change may bring insecurity. It can bring criticism or endanger that which is profitable or convenient for us. In Ibsen's play *An Enemy of the People,* Dr. Stockman, the medical officer for the baths of a resort town, finds that they are polluted with typhoid germs and are dangerous. The exposure of this problem may ruin the business of the town and is resisted by the authorities. Accepting the danger would mean revolutionary change. It was easier then (not in a disease-conscious age like our own!) to ignore the menace and brand the doctor as "an enemy of the people" than to make the needed changes. Change the idiom to nuclear power and the present controversy over safety versus needed energy and it becomes a modern problem. We would rather dismiss from our minds the possible danger of nuclear waste than to change our habits in the use of energy.

We may become so accustomed to that which needs changing that we are no longer aware of it. A number of years ago we lived in a small town in the East Texas oil field where there were many small gasoline–producing plants known as "cracking plants." Their fumes were noxious. We grew so accustomed to the odor after a short time that we never smelled it unless we had been away and returned to the place. We can grow so accustomed to the world with its prejudice, its violence and its basic selfishness that we become indifferent and change is difficult to effect. We can live so close to our own sins that we become unaware of them.

We are reluctant to face evils in our lives that should be changed. I once visited a man whose life was threatened by alcoholism. I gave him every opportunity to discuss his problem, but he never did, and eventually a life on the whole generous and open to human need was destroyed. It was difficult for him to say, "I am wrong," or "I am at fault," or "I need help." In recent years since the Watergate scandal there has been a spectacle of a long line of government officials, including the President of the United States, rationalizing their conduct, constructing excuses about their obvious wrongdoing, seldom saying, "I was wrong." People can confess the sins of others readily and refuse utterly to admit their own failures. It takes courage to admit that we are neglectful parents, inconsiderate husbands, insensitive wives, unconcerned employees or employers, unworthy citizens, unfaithful church members. We would rather make our excuses. Tragedy can result. In Arthur Miller's play *After the Fall,* Quentin says to his wife Maggie:

> You eat those pills like power.... If you could only say, "I have been cruel," this frightening room would open. If you could say, "I have been kicked around, but I have been just as inexcusably vicious to others, called my husband an idiot in public, I have been utterly selfish despite my generosity, I have been hurt by a long line of men but I have cooperated with my persecutors.

But we cannot say the words any more than this unfortunate woman could say them, and change is denied. The past cannot be cut off, discarded like a pair of worn-out shoelaces or yesterday's paper. Disposal is not so easy. A person who tries to change without a realistic appraisal of his liabilities may find himself in great difficulty. Memories may torment. Malicious and hostile feelings are not conquered through any demand that they depart.

We can be locked into binding patterns of behavior, blind to our sins, reluctant to face them. Actually our problem in making changes may be none of these. We may be quite happy with our lives, content in our own selfishness, and so unwilling to make changes. John wrote that "men loved darkness rather than the light."

> ... every one who does evil hates the light, and does not come to
> the light, lest his deeds should be exposed. (John 3:20)

To a certain extent we all share in this condemnation.

Change must come, but sometimes it is held back by the ways in which it is sought. The method determines the product. It must be constructive change, based on good will, understanding and faith. There is a temptation to avoid the long, hard road of sacrificial love and kindly persuasion and resort to violent means to make a new world. Harsh and repressive measures to preserve order are proposed and practiced, but they have a tendency to build violence into the system and encourage its use. Punishments with no remedial possibilities, such as capital punishment, have no capacity to bring constructive change and in general brutalize society. From a different point of view, when people are forced into accepted patterns and denied justice it is a temptation to see revolutionary violence as an answer to such oppression. There are strong arguments against such measures.

Violence leads only to further chaos and suffering. In his novel *The Honorary Consul,* Graham Greene addresses the problem of whether injustice, in this case the oppression of a dictator of a South American country, can be remedied through armed rebellion. A priest joins the revolutionaries and helps in the kidnapping of a supposed dignitary in order to obtain the release of other revolutionaries who are in prison. It sounds like a plot lifted from the front page of a current newspaper. The result is the crushing of the mistaken idealists, the deaths of the priest and of a man of good will who had tried to bring reconciliation. Violence merely aggravated a bad situation.

Recourse to violence is really an admission that problems cannot be solved. In her novel *Wait Until Evening,* Henrietta Buckmaster writes: "I think the real sickness is not so much the violence as the belief that nothing works, nothing is to be trusted" (page 139). Harry Emerson Fosdick once said that the evil of war is not simply in death and destruction, but in the fostering of the idea that any kind of violence solves anything. Foundations of trust and understanding are required for any change that is constructive and fulfilling. Violence has no way of building such foundations. It calls for the rejection of some of our fellows and encourages hate and a desire for revenge. If God loves all men, as we are taught, then it is our calling as Christians to love as God has loved, forgive as God has forgiven. Violence makes this impossible. Once started, it is hard to stop. It provokes more violence. The feud of the two families in Shakespeare's *Romeo and Juliet* could never be stopped until someone broke the circle of hate. With that, change came.

Repentance is a vital part of the dynamic of change. It includes facing failure honestly. It is not a once-for-all proposition, but includes repeated self-examination. It is more than admitting that we are wrong. It involves sorrow for evil committed and for all that we have failed to do. It is sorrow for the corporate sins of the world in which we are involved, for evil conditions for which we must share at least a part of the blame.

The realism of repentance is tested in several ways. Our sorrow should bring us to the place where we admit our own emptiness, our helplessness without the grace of God. This is a negative test, but there is a positive one. Repentance should bring us to a change in thinking and action, a new direction for living. We would not be able to face the desolation of repentance if we did not have a faith in Christ which assures forgiveness and at the same time supplies the goal and dynamic for a new way of life.

Dealing with guilt is a part of the problem. Facing the evils of our own lives and of society and finding help in forgiveness does not mean that we should be preoccupied with them. If the sense of guilt persists life will be poisoned by it, made ineffective. The mind that is cluttered with self-defeating memories is apt to repeat mistakes. If I have dealt unjustly with someone, no good purpose is served by remembering my fault and seeking constantly to make amends. Forgiveness must lead to forgetfulness.

Suppose evil lingers in deeply ingrained habits, of malicious speech, for instance. Do I conquer by saying, "I shall not do this," concentrating on fighting a bad habit? A better strategy is the formation of a new habit to take the place of the old, a search for good things to say of others and opportunities to praise. Unfortunately new habits do not come at will. The inner resources are lacking.

We need the will, the abiding impulse to change, to find a freedom from old failures. It does not come by compulsive striving. We fail miserably that way. The answer is in letting God handle things, trusting in the Spirit to bring fruition in our lives. In the apostolic writings there is evidence everywhere of new life thrilled with the joy of a great deliverance; new life conscious of powers not its own, of new motivations, of new outlooks; a life in constant change as it responded to problems met. How did this come about?

Theodore Ferris tells of a man who was a drug addict who wanted to be free. He joined a therapeutic program and found himself bewildered. Counselors were talking about *principles,* and he thought that meant a guy who ran a school. They spoke of *values* and he could only think of the prices you pay at the stores. When they spoke of *convictions* he could only think of that as being what you got before a judge. So he was bewildered. But after a time he discovered the meanings of those terms and he had the good fortune to meet a person who had the principles they were talking about. He resolved to be like that person and it was the turning point in his life. Others have found inspiration in a person. Tennessee Williams became a playwright after seeing Nazimova in Ibsen's *Ghosts.* Abraham Lincoln received his love of the English language from a Dartmouth student. People have been able to see what Christ was like from observing those who have loved him. We learn more from people and their actions than we do from words. When we know Christ intimately we become new creatures. We learn to hate the debased lives we have been living. The sins which crucified him become detestable to us. He not only teaches us how to live but gives us the power to change, to turn from doing our will to following God's will. We serve him with a new spirit, not as slaves, but sons.

Is change possible for people like this who have found Christ? It is not only possible but observable. In race relations in America there have been changes in rights secured, attitudes transformed, relationships improved. In a discussion group recently in which there were both black and white and members of a variety of Christian churches and a Jewish synagogue, it was the unanimous opinion that human relationships in our city had changed remarkably in the past decade. Understandings and actions are possible which would have been impossible previously. Not only have there been alterations in society but individuals have come to a different point of view. A woman confided to me that people were irritated with their pastor when he endeavored to change racial practices in the church in the sixties but that they now knew that he acted correctly. Redemptive change had come.

My father was reared in a society strictly segregated. His values were rooted in that way of life. He read widely, however, and discussed openly the problems involved. At the same time his life in the church became meaningful. He wrestled with the problem of race prejudice with the knowledge that he would offend some of his friends if he changed his views. In the process he came to a new conviction and a new relationship with black people. As early as the forties and fifties he made changes in his practices, championing the rights of those denied privileges. Through the grace of God change came.

The new man is incomplete until he directs his energies toward the making of a new world. Change is going on in the world, constructive, life-giving change as well as that which destroys. Christians must be a part of that constructive change. The sin which makes change necessary is not merely an individual, private reality, but a social and historical fact. It takes form as an absence of love and brotherhood among men as well as a conflict between men and God. It is evident in oppressive structures, exploitation of human beings, and domination of peoples, races and social classes. The heartbreaking violence which is a part of daily life, in which men often turn against and destroy those who are endeavoring to help them, has its roots in frustration, grinding poverty, prejudice, fear, hate and greed. The creation of a new man in Christ involves a struggle against such misery and injustice. The saving process embraces the whole life of man and all of human history. Only thus can it be true to the magnitude of Christ's salvation. "God so loved the *world* that he gave his only Son."

CHAPTER SEVEN

Getting Together

Some of the most painful experiences of my life have been times of misunderstanding with others which were difficult to clear up. In one case I made a statement in a sermon concerning atrocities in Vietnam which offended a member of the church. He thought that I had been unfair in the charge made and told me so. I felt that I had simply told the truth. We refrained from discussing the matter. There was an estrangement as a result that was never completely overcome. We should have done something about it. The memory of a flawed relationship remains.

Something that Jesus said reminds me of my neglect in this matter. He was talking about killing and the fact that one who kills is liable to judgment, and he added that one who is angry with his brother is also liable to judgment. Insult and hate rate even worse penalties. He offered a remedy for such a problem:

> "So if you are offering your gift at the altar, and there remember that your brother has something against you, leave your gift there before the altar and go; first be reconciled to your brother, and then come and offer your gift." (Matthew 5:23–24)

Jesus was saying that making peace with God is conditioned on making peace with our brothers. Reconciliation with our fellows has a vital connection with reconciliation with God. Our human estrangements get in the way of our fellowship with God. They do not cut us off completely. God's love is stronger than that. We are told that nothing can separate us from the love of God. He forgives and accepts us in spite of our failures. But the obligation remains. Paul wrote to the Romans (12:18): "If possible, so far as it depends upon you, live peaceably with all." There are several aspects of our broken relationships which make reconciliation difficult but necessary.

Guilt is one of these. I found it impossible to have a completely open relationship with my friend who was unhappy with me. There was a stiffness and formality about our relationship. We kept our distance. One of my impediments, seen in the perspective of the years, was that I felt guilty about offending him. Perhaps it could not have been avoided. Differences of opinion over the war were heated. My condemnation may have served only to aggravate rather than persuade. This is not to say that we should not have strong convictions and express them. We do not help each other to grow simply by remaining silent, but we have to learn to "speak the truth in love." When we fail to do that and guilt overtakes us fellowship is frustrated.

People who fail to work out their differences in love may go further than bruised feelings and distant relationships. Open hostility may result. Some years ago it was my unhappy responsibility to chair a commission sent to hear the problems of a church in trouble and help them to find a solution. The minister and his officers were at odds and there was disharmony in the whole congregation. We had an open hearing, which proved to be a mistake. All those aggrieved poured out their hate and the more moderate kept silent. We escaped the problem by having new officers elected and asking the pastor to move to another church. It was a poor solution that created more animosities. Eventually peace was restored, but the struggle hurt the church.

Fear is another factor in broken relationships. A man had lost his wife after a long life together. As we sat in his living room he told me something about her which helped to explain her unwillingness to be involved in any sort of fellowship.

"Her life was dominated by fear," he said.
"Of what was she afraid?" I asked.
"She was afraid of everything. She was afraid about her health, her financial security, afraid of people, afraid of what was happening in the world. Fear ruined her life."

I think of how many I know like this woman, people terrified by the world, by real or fancied threats to their security, not knowing the comfort of a fellowship that could support and assure. I visited often an older woman who lives alone in a house which is beyond her ability to maintain. She confines herself to one cluttered room and trusts only a handful of people. Once active and helpful, she is now alienated from society. I thought also of a college girl who said she could not trust people over thirty, that they lied and could not be trusted. How had such distrust been spawned?

An unwillingness to be involved with others may grow out of our fear of being hurt in the process. Mark Gerzon in his study of youth dissent, *The Whole World Is Watching,* describes his high school days in the late sixties:

> The last thing we wanted was to be concerned, or open, or involved, or serious. We wanted to be cool, detached—and successful. We wanted to be tough—which we thought meant *not caring.* We had not learned . . . that real toughness is *being able to care.* (p. 49)

The things we fail to do by remaining aloof weaken fellowship.

On the other hand the achievements of others may bring jealousy and covetousness. A doctor describes his patients in all walks of life as seemingly "engaged in a marathon race, their eager faces distorted by strain, their eyes focused not on their goal but on each other with a mixture of hate, envy and admiration. They would all like to stop but dare not as long as others are running."

The Letter of James helps us to understand this disruptive tension:

> What causes wars, and what causes fightings among you? Is it not your passions that are at war in your members? You desire and do not have; so you kill. And you covet and cannot obtain, so you fight and wage war. (James 4:1)

A present-day economist came to the same conclusion in his book *Small Is Beautiful.* E. F. Schumacher wrote:

> If human vices such as greed and envy are systematically cultivated, the inevitable result is nothing less than a collapse of intelligence. A man driven by greed or envy loses

the power of seeing things as they really are, of seeing things in their roundness and wholeness, and his very successes become failures. If whole societies become infected by these vices, they may indeed achieve astonishing things but they become increasingly incapable of solving the most elementary problems of everyday existance. (p. 29)

And surely the most pressing problem we have is that of living together in peace.

We are driven apart in many ways—by guilt, hostility, fear, indifference and greed. We must find a way of getting together and this means that we must first of all get together with God. Reconciliation with our fellows depends on reconciliation with God. The deepest reason for disharmony is the fact that in some way we have blocked God out of our lives. That blockage has poisoned all of life. We cut off the source of love in God and become strangers to one another.

Jesus told a story in Luke 15 which illustrates both our need and God's answer to it. It was about a younger son of a family who seemed to have very little in common with his father and was restive with his brother. Bored with his home and wanting to lead his own life, he asks for his share of the father's property. The freedom from responsibility in a distant land is freedom to waste everything that he has. He finds himself in a worse servitude than he ever knew at home. Since almost nothing is worse than feeding pigs among strangers who have no interest in him, he resolves to return and accept service with his father. His welcome home is beyond his expectation, joyful acceptance with every evidence of love. This is our story. We renounce the relationships of love and trust that God has provided. If we repent of our willfulness and stupidity and return we find that God still has a place for us, that all is not lost, that we can begin again. Reconciliation is restoration to the family of God.

Paul gives another picture of reconciliation in Romans 5. Here we are not merely rebellious sons who refuse fellowship. We are enemies, hostile to God and quite helpless to do anything about our plight. "While we were yet sinners Christ died for us." It might seem reasonable for Christ to die for his friends, but for his enemies? for criminals? for the scum of the earth? This seems too much. Make it as impossible as we can according to our standards; it is impossible to fathom the love of God for his children. His sacrificial love in Christ is sufficient to overcome the worst of our enmities, relieve us of the burden of our guilt, still our fears, awaken us out of our indifference, give us new goals for living. The free gift of a reconciled life is ours through Jesus Christ. In Ephesians 2 Christ is called "our peace." He has "broken down the dividing wall of hostility," brought our hostility to an end. We are no longer "strangers and sojourners," but "fellow citizens with the saints and members of the household of God." Reconciliation is God's achievement, not ours.

One Sunday morning I received a telephone call from an old friend. He told me that he had flown into the city the previous evening and wanted to talk to me about professing his faith as a Christian. Could I see him at the church school hour and help him to understand what it meant? He was a man in his late thirties and had attended church for years but had never confessed his faith. He had come because I happened to be the only minister that he knew well. What could I say that would give him the heart of the whole matter? I told him of reconciliation, of the removal through Christ of what separates us from God and our fellows. We discussed that separation, the sin which destroys loving relationships, the selfishness which makes us prefer our own good to the good of others and our own ways to the ways and will of God. I spoke of the wall this creates, isolating us from God. But through his sacrificial love on the cross Christ removed that wall and inspired us to trust him. God accepts us and forgives us. Fellowship with God and our fellows is made possible. The way is opened for a new life of love and service. That was as simple as I could make it. My friend had been exposed to all these things many times, but on that day he accepted them as his own. He returned home to become a valuable member of his church.

The new man in Christ, the reconciled person, can rejoice in the fact that he is no longer a stranger but a person accepted. His privilege brings an obligation. Writing to the Corinthians Paul says that God "through Christ reconciled us to himself and gave us the ministry of reconciliation (2 Corinthians 5:18). Our salvation becomes real for us as we accept the role of reconciler in the world. We are set free from old hates, resented wrongs, suspicions and fears, and the walls of misunderstanding which separate us from others. This emancipation is a lifelong process, but along the way we have a new role. We are "ambassadors for Christ, God making his appeal through us" (2 Corinthians 5:20). It is a challenging assignment. As ambassadors for Christ we are not to punish those who disagree with us or displease us. We are to forgive as we have been forgiven. The world is waiting for that. A little child, guilty of misbehaving, found himself in a room surrounded by adults who were stern in their disapproval to let him know how wrong he was. He looked at his parents, relatives, friends, one by one, in the hope of finding someone who would relent; and when he found no sympathy he burst into tears, crying out, "Oh, won't someone forgive me?" He expressed a need as elemental as our need for bread. We can fill that need through God's grace. To be an ambassador of reconciliation is to learn to forgive.

It is also the role of the reconciler to lead others to exercise forgiveness and build bridges of understanding and trust. When I was a student in theological seminary I was asked to go to a church for the summer and preach while the congregation looked for a new pastor. When I arrived I was met by the clerk of session of the church and told that the church was divided over the leaving of a pastor under pressure, a man who was disliked by a large segment of the congregation and liked by others. It was discouraging news for an inexperienced student pastor, but since I was already there and there was nowhere else to go, I stayed. It was amazing how the summer went. It was really one of the happiest times of my life. I preached, conducted a vacation church school, visited, listened when someone wanted to talk and did not enter into the controversy. The work of reconciliation and weathering of the storm for that church was the labor of that clerk of session who had confided his concern when I arrived. He listened, encouraged, did not take sides, and became a peacemaker for his people. It was largely due to his influence that the church stayed together and later became one of the stronger churches of its denomination. Afterward, I thought of his method. He was never judgmental, never blamed the people for their mistakes, sympathized with their differences and conflicting loyalties. In all this he never appeased them, but encouraged them to remain true to Christ and to face their problem in his spirit. He was a minister of reconciliation.

The essential role for the Christian reconciler is that of a servant. Paul wrote to the Philippians (chapter 2) that they should have the mind and spirit of Christ, who "emptied himself, taking the form of a servant, being born in the likeness of men." We are the servant people of a servant Lord. If the Creator of the universe took this humble role to save men, to reconcile them to one another, we can do no less than identify with our neighbors' problems, share their concerns, help them to look at their differences reasonably and let the love of Christ flow from our lives into theirs.

The task is larger than we may think. "God was in Christ reconciling the *world* to himself, not counting their trespasses against them, and entrusting to us the message of reconciliation" (2 Corinthians 5:19). God's purpose in Christ is to "reconcile to himself all things, whether on earth or in heaven, making peace by the blood of the cross" (Colossians 1:20). We are a part of that purpose. Reconciliation means not simply the healing of the wounds of the past but the opening up of a new future for the world. It is our call to be the instruments of God in the realization of that purpose.

There is a role both for the individual Christian and for the church in the healing of the divisions of our world. It means intelligent action to remove, so far as we are able, the causes of conflict— the degrading poverty, the ignorance and neglect, the injustice and exploitation, the prejudice, hate and fear that tear people apart. On the positive side it means the building of relationships of trust and confidence, becoming ourselves those who can be trusted. It is the slow process of working through complex problems with the love of Christ and the guidance of his Spirit. There is a place for the resources for reconciliation of our faith in the arbitration of labor disputes, the working out of the problems of the use of energy and the settlement around a conference table of an international dispute.

For a number of years I had the privilege of being a member of an interchurch committee studying the economic life of our country and making recommendations concerning the solutions to some of its problems. The committee was composed of leaders of industry and of labor, professors of economics, members of the faculties of universities and theological seminaries, bankers, engineers, writers in the field and a few ministers. Opinions of these people were varied, but they had one thing in common, a loyalty to Christ and to his church. The discussions were often heated, but they brought us closer together. They produced insights that were valuable for the whole church. I thought of the group as a fellowship of reconciliation. We were exercising the ministry of reconciliation as we looked at our differences in the light of the gospel. We need not be a part of such a committee to accomplish the same ends. There are opportunities all around us to render the same service if we take our ministry seriously.

CHAPTER EIGHT

We Need Each Other

One of my earliest memories is of being a member of a church in a small town in Texas. I remember the pew our family occupied, as well as the faces of the people who sat in the pews around us. We knew so much about those people. They were like members of the family. It was from that pew that I rose one evening during a revival meeting and answered an invitation to confess my faith in Christ and "join the church." Of course I was already a part of that church. I always had been. I cannot remember ever being a stranger in the church. Being a part of the church was like being a part of my own family. I knew very little of what I was doing then. I learned a great deal about the implications of that decision in my subsequent experiences in the church.

Memories are clear of a teacher who was patient in her training of a class of restless boys, who taught us the elements of our faith. The choir offered an opportunity for service. There were other enriching experiences. I attended a prayer meeting with my grandmother on Wednesday evenings with a handful of people. We had an elderly doctor who was always there and prayed in polished phrases, usually the same ones each week, something about being faithful in the "church militant" until we reached the "church triumphant," a prayer not always answered in the lives of some of us! The fact that such experiences are so vivid in my memory speaks of their helpful influence. It was in that church that I talked to my pastor about becoming a minister, and, after years of education, it was there that I was ordained a minister. What I recall most is the congregation's interest in me and their faith in my possibilities. There was always a warm welcome when I returned home and financial support when it was needed. I needed them and I think that they needed me. We needed each other.

All through life I have belonged to groups that I left behind—civic clubs, service organizations, cultural groups and other voluntary associations. Each had its purpose and appeal. Each met in some way my need for community. Every fellowship we have is a gift of God's grace, for he created us to live and work together. The church was different. When I moved to some new situation I never left the church behind. Wherever I went there was an extension of that church family I knew in my youth, with common interests, a common history, common practices and common beliefs. It was a case of "one body and one Spirit . . . one hope . . . one Lord, one faith, one baptism, one God and Father of us all, who is above all and through all and in all" (Ephesians 4:4–6). I came to realize that the faith I had with all its associations was not a private possession but the property of a community. What mattered was not so much what belonged to me as to what I belonged—Christ's church—and to whom I belonged—Christ the Lord of the church.

Since the publication of Alex Haley's book *Roots* there has been a widespread interest in tracing family trees, discovering our ancestry and finding our origins. It is a useful interest, not only in the satisfaction of curiosity but in establishing the identity of the individual involved. Many are not happy as persons with a vague background. We need to know who we are. There is just as important a need to know the background of our faith, our spiritual origins. Behind us there are many generations of people who maintained Christian beliefs, ventured out in their thinking and spiritual development, took the church to the ends of the earth and ministered to human needs in the name of Christ. Our Christian faith is more than the result of a present encounter with our Lord. It is a rich heritage, a gift to us from those who have gone before us. We owe a great debt to the pioneers of the faith who "looked forward to the city which has foundations, whose builder and maker is God" (Hebrews 11:10). This is what the writer of Hebrews taught when he said we were "surrounded by so great a cloud of witnesses" (Hebrews 12:1). Our common debt to the past makes us one in Christ.

Not long ago my wife and I went to a small college town in North Carolina to be with my brother who had lost his wife. Leukemia had taken her life after a short illness. Her death was a shock to the community where she had been an officer in the church, a teacher in the public schools and an active participant in college affairs. We were impressed by the way in which the people of the church anticipated every need of the family by taking care of food, lodging for those who had come from out of town and every other sort of arrangement as well as giving sympathy and encouragement. This happens under many circumstances with many different groups, but these folk did more. They were able to strengthen faith because they shared that faith in Christ with us. Jesus said, "Blessed are they that mourn for they shall be comforted." His comfort often comes through such a shared faith. We need each other when the crises of life come.

Some people have difficulty making friends. I visited an elderly woman lately who described her loneliness. She had no close relatives, no person to whom she could confide her problems. At least she had the advantage of living in a congregate facility for the elderly provided by our church, but a person can be lonely although surrounded by people. She offers us a challenge. Perhaps she will find what she needs in the fellowship of love and service our church has endeavored to create. Our facility is not an impersonal dwelling place for older people but a place where each one is treated as an individual and given opportunities for self-development and the making of friends.

Loneliness affects people of all ages. A fellowship for single people in our city has drawn together people from several congregations who need more than the fellowship of those sharing their work; they need the friendship of those who share their faith and ideals. A young man visited me at my office. We often have people who need money, food or some assistance of the same kind. This one was different. He needed to talk to someone. Would I listen to him for a time? There came a long recital of misfortunes and a confession that he had no friends. He too offered a challenge. He had a need difficult to supply, but he had looked to the church for help. He sensed what the church ought to be. Jesus called his disciples "friends." In his last hours he gave his disciples a new commandment:

> "that you love one another; even as I have loved you that you also love one another. By this all men will know that you are my disciples, if you have love for one another." (John 13:34–35)

The distinguishing mark of the church before the world is the love that members have for one another and for all human beings. John wrote, "We know that we have passed out of death into life, because we love the brethren" (1 John 3:14). The building of a true fellowship is an assurance both to ourselves and to the world that salvation is a reality. We need each other. The answer to that need may come in various ways.

How many different kinds of people can be found in a Christian church! In ours, for instance, there are groups who are more secure in traditional lectures in their church school classes. Other groups like to discuss the issues of the day or look at the Scriptures from a fresh viewpoint. There are people in both groups who have different opinions on questions and are free to air their views. They learn to listen to each other and often help each other to think more clearly. They have something personal to share. We have people from many different backgrounds. This is the way it should be. We do not need to be alike, a collection of carbon copies. We do need acceptance, affirmation as individuals. The church is called "the household of God" (Ephesians 2:19). A human family may have members with many different qualities and styles of life and yet be a fellowship of love because each person is respected and valued for what he is. We need each other's acceptance and respect.

A church in Richmond, Virginia, had a recreation center for black young people in an old store building in a slum area. The equipment was meager—a few games, a battered old pool table and a well-used ping-pong table. When I was there as a visitor one evening the place was full of teen-agers, music was blaring from a phonograph and people were waiting in line for every game. I stepped outside for a few minutes and found a group of smaller children watching for an opportunity to slip in. They should have been at home. They had had their opportunity to play in the afternoon, but they were not satisfied. Their presence was evidence of their need. The church was trying to meet that need. The life of that church was reshaped as it discovered the shape of the need in the neighborhood that it served. This is so often true. The life of the church I serve has been affected by a ministry to alcoholics in a "halfway house," a summer program for slum children, a ministry to the elderly in providing living accommodations and "meals on wheels" for the handicapped who live at home. Through the support of this church wells will be dug in Africa to bring relief from drought and make agriculture possible. Medical clinics will be placed in remote areas in Zaire that will make treatment more available to the sick. Missionaries are being supported who serve in a hospital in Korea and who are helping to build a better life for people in Africa. The variety of efforts by churches to give "a more abundant life" to the people of the earth is virtually endless—hospitals in Mexico and Haiti, agricultural missions in a poverty-stricken area of Honduras, schools in Japan, pioneer churches in the newly-settled frontier of Brazil, to name a few.

Christ claimed that his ministry through the Spirit was "to preach good news to the poor," "to proclaim release to the captives," "recovery of sight to the blind," " to set at liberty those that are oppressed." It would follow that those who are his followers will witness best as they work with the Spirit in his work of liberation. Community is best realized where Christ is, among the desperately needy people of the earth. Sensitivity to the needs of our neighbors and an active effort to meet those needs are necessary ingredients for Christian fellowship. We may have a great concern about the needs of mankind but lack a structure through which the needs may be met. The church provides that structure and the faith and love to make it effective. Through the cooperation of denominations resources are pooled, overlapping avoided, personnel shared. Through such efforts millions hear the gospel by radio; hunger is fought through "One Great Hour of Sharing" at Easter; millions are learning to read all over the world. We need each other to make service effective.

Paul used a number of word pictures to describe the church in the world. Each parable speaks of our need for each other's fellowship and support when comfort, forgiveness, strength and acceptance are needed or opportunities for service are offered. As has been noted, the church has been called the "household of God"—a family. Many of us have experienced it as that. As members of a family there are ties which bind us together. There are some problems with the picture. Human families are so limited in their scope. They go only so far. Sometimes they are ruptured and their members alienated. Members of a family may destroy one another. The church as we see it may be just as imperfect, but what substitute do we have for it? Infidelities may mar its life, but the need for it remains. The church as the household of God has this comfort, that God's reconciliation in Christ is the source of its peace and that its members "have access in one Spirit to the Father" (Ephesians 2:18). The hope for the church is in the Christ who rules it and who said that "the powers of death shall not prevail against it."

Imagine a family with no limits, into which "strangers and sojourners" are welcomed, where no person needs to feel that he is an outsider, where there are possibilities of salvation for the whole family of man—that is the church in the world.

We built a new educational building for our church recently and I watched its construction with interest. Foundations were laid; the steel structure was erected; the bricks were laid. Each part had its place in the building and none could have been omitted. Paul was thinking of such a structure when he described the church as "a holy temple in the Lord; in whom you also are built into it for a dwelling place of God in the Spirit" (Ephesians 2:22). Each member is a part of the building. He bears his share of the stresses and strains and carries his part of the support. If this does not happen the church is weakened. Christ gave a great responsibility to his disciples when he said that he would build his church on their faith as Peter had expressed it (Matt.16:18). We need each other as we build Christ's church in the world.

A patient in a hospital was discussing with me his long illness. Cancer of the pituitary gland had required a difficult operation. He had been in and out of the hospital for years. There were many unfortunate complications, for that small gland controls some of our most important bodily functions. Paul knew little of the glands, but he did know that this complex body of ours is composed of many organs, each with its particular and indispensable purpose for the most part. He compared the church with such a body, making it more in its essential nature than a voluntary association or a formal organization. He thought of it as an orgnic whole, with the life and effectiveness of each part depending on all the rest.

Is Paul's description of the church as a body a picture of what the church ought to be if its members fulfilled their functions perfectly and were bound together by ideal relationships? Hardly. In his first letter to the Corinthians Paul describes those to whom he wrote as "men of the flesh" and "babes in Christ." They were seriously divided in their loyalties to various leaders. Their moral lives were scandalous. Personal antagonisms made some sue others in the courts. All kinds of family and sex problems plagued them. They had offended each other seriously through insistence on narrow customs about food and drink. Division over social status even affected the celebration of the feast which should draw all Christians together, the Lord's Supper. They had problems about faith and doctrine, about the debated custom of speaking in tongues and the hope of the Resurrection. One can scarcely imagine a church more torn with strife and division.

Some of the churchmen of that day, convinced that this was not really the church would have been glad to reject the Corinthian Christians; but Paul called these people "the Body of Christ." His most moving description of the dependence of Christians on one another and their responsibilties to each other is written concerning them. He did not hesitate to condemn their sins, but insisted that in spite of all its blemishes this was indeed the body of Christ in the world. The body might be sick and its members uncooperative, but it was still the church.

He saw the members of the body as diverse, having a great variety of gifts; but because of differences the members could not disown one another, as Christians are tempted to do, for they were as interdependent as the organs of the human body. No part could claim that all others should be as it was. How peculiar a body would be if it were all ear, or eye or nose! The early Christians could no more dispense with some members than a body could reject the liver or the lungs and stay alive. Even weaker members, lacking perhaps in moral stamina, ability, even love, were indispensable. Each was valuable in his own right. Each should take care of the others. If one suffered, all suffered. When one was honored all rejoiced. Each had his particular task to fulfill according to the gifts given him by the Spirit of God.

This description of the church as a body speaks to many of our human needs:

Our need to be different and yet able to work together.

Our need to be included, not rejected.

Our need to be valued for what we are with no comparisons.

Our need to exercise whatever abilities God has given us.

Our need for one gift above all, essential to the functioning of our life together—love. There has never been a better description of that love than 1 Corinthians 13.

We are joined not through our needs but through the answer to those needs. It is not togetherness in itself that saves us but a mighty force that breaks down the barriers that keep us apart, a divine love which inspires all our loves, a power of the Spirit which unites us. As Paul wrote to the Corinthians:

> ... by one Spirit we were all baptized into one body—Jews or Greeks, slave or free—and all were made to drink of one Spirit.
> (1 Corinthians 12:13)

I have been talking to a young couple about the baptism of their first child, who is just a few weeks old. I am trying to help them to understand how important this step is. Sometimes the baptism of an infant is regarded as no more than a customary routine, but it has a deep meaning and a significance for all of life. In baptism we claim a promise that God has made to us and to our children. On the day of Pentecost Peter said to the crowd:

> "Repent, and be baptized every one of you in the name of Jesus Christ for the forgiveness of your sins; and you shall receive the gift of the Holy Spirit. For the promise is to you and to your children and to all that are far off, every one whom the Lord our God calls to him." (Acts 2:38–39)

Baptism signifies our cleansing from sin, our renewal through the work of Christ. As Paul wrote, it is a work of God's Spirit in which the person is stamped as God's child, a member of God's family. It looks foward to the time when the child shall make his own decision and confess his own faith in Christ. But in the meantime he is not a stranger in the household of God but a member of the family. In baptism pledges are made by the parents and by the congregation which joins these parents in their vows. Something happens in the lives of all concerned and in the life of the whole church when a child receives baptism or an adult chooses to be baptized. It is told of Martin Luther that when he went through his darkest hours in bringing the Reformation into being he would comfort himself by saying, "I have been baptized." His baptism testified to the world that he belonged to Christ and that he was a member of Christ's body in the world, the church, and, being that, nothing could destroy him. Baptism speaks not only of the fact that we are dependent on God but also that we need each other. Through baptism we are a part of a fellowship empowered by God.

Some of the happiest and best remembered times in the life of our family have been our vacations, opportunities to be away from the ordinary routines of life together. We learned to know each other better during these annual excursions. We found more time to do things together, read, think and worship. These times helped us to develop a family spirit which remains with us. Our children have their own homes and children now but we still vacation together. Whether we were at a mountain cabin, a campsite in some national park or forest, or a seashore cottage, we had a custom of having grace said at meals in a variety of ways. Sometimes we would sing the familiar "Doxology," or Johnny Appleseed's happy song of thanksgiving or any one of a dozen other songs, one in Spanish. Sometimes one of the family, child or adult, would lead in prayer. Our best moments of fellowship were around a table, at a meal. We seemed to be closer there to each other and to God.

When our Lord wanted to bring his disciples together before he left them he gathered them around a table. It was to celebrate a very old feast, the Passover, the remembrance then of the liberation of the Jewish people 1,500 years before. Several meaningful things happened that evening. Christ took a basin and towel and washed his disciples' feet, teaching them that humble service is basic in our fellowship as Christians. He reminded them that they would always be helpless without his inspiration and strength. He was the vine and they were the branches. Cut off from him they would be helpless. He broke bread and said that the breaking of bread was to remind them of the breaking of his body for their sakes. He gave them a cup of wine which stood for his blood, shed in sacrificial love. The Lord's Supper continues to tell us that we cannot live together as Christians without our Lord. As we remember him in the Supper shared with other Christians we are drawn together in a living fellowship.

Many memories come to me as I join my fellow Christians around the Lord's table—of communing with a group of young people on a mountaintop around a campfire on a summer's evening, of receiving communion on my knees in a great church, of serving communion to the sick with only a few present or to a multitude in an inspiring service. Always it is the same Supper, the same Lord and the same Church—his Church, his Body in the world.

CHAPTER NINE

The Power of Commitment

A chairman was needed for the Every Member Canvass, the annual drive to raise the funds for our church's operation. It was a demanding task for we were trying to build new church school rooms to replace some temporary wooden ones that were past being usable. The budget would have to be increased about thirty percent to make this possible. Finally one of the deacons agreed to serve. He was a businessman with many responsibilities. Taking this assignment would mean a heavy drain on his time and energies. Yet he committed himself to the task. Why?

He would probably have found it difficult to answer that question. Our motives are not always clear to us and are usually quite mixed. There may have been a desire on his part to exercise power, to manage things. He was an able administrator. There is an appeal in such a task that challenges. This one did. To be a success in the mission we undertake gives a certain inner satisfaction. It has rewards also in the applause of others. All these factors may have induced him to undertake this job for his church.

There may have been some things that discouraged his acceptance. In the face of the demands, which included much planning and many meetings, he could have said that he was too busy. He was already active in the church in other ways. He could have said to himself that no one ever became popular asking for money, and regardless of how great his effort it would soon be forgotten. There would be the problem of getting cooperation from the other officers.

He could fail, which would be a blow to his self-esteem. If he became too involved he might be trapped, expected to do other things that he did not relish.

I have no idea whether these unpleasant possibilities occurred to him. At any rate they did not sway him. There were reasons for him to dedicate himself to this task which were far stronger. The need of the church was obvious. With an inner city location it would have little future without adequate facilities. It would have to make a strong effort in this campaign or die. Family ties may have played a part in his decision. His father had been a minister and he was grateful for his heritage. He wanted a vigorous church for his family. But above and beyond all these things there was a loyalty to Christ. Without this it is doubtful if he would have overcome the obstacles that could have blocked his decision. Our commitments are made in the context of conflicting motives and pressures, but some controlling loyalty makes all the difference. "The love of Christ controls us," wrote Paul to the Corinthians (2 Corinthians 5:14). Incidentally, the deacon's work was successful. He challenged the people by agreeing to double his own contribution and led others to commit themselves by his example.

Commitment means entrusting ourselves—our money, our time, our strength, any extension of ourselves—to be used for a purpose. It implies a confidence in the cause, organization or person to which that commitment is made. It is an active expression of faith. Paul described Christian commitment when he wrote to the Corinthians about the wholehearted generosity of the churches of Macedonia toward the needs of other Christians, "taking part in the relief of the saints—and this, not as we expected, but first gave themselves to the Lord and to us by the will of God" (2 Corinthians 8:4–5). Salvation is not complete without it—this entrusting ourselves, all we are and all we have to Christ. It is a leap of faith in which we ask him to use us for his purpose.

We learn very soon that there are conflicts in calls to commitment which give us trouble. Jesus was aware of these. "No one can serve two masters," he said. "You cannot serve God and mammon" (Matthew 6:24). Mammon means anything we possess. It is a question of our highest allegiance. Are we committed to what we own or to God? Speaking of the paying of taxes, he said, "Render therefore to Caesar the things that are Caesar's and to God the things that are God's" (Matthew 22:21). There are duties we owe to the state but over and above them are the things we owe to God. One of Christ's sayings that is hardest for us to understand is this: "If any one comes to me and does not hate his own father and mother and wife and children and brothers and sisters, yes, and even his own life, he cannot be my disciple" (Luke 14:26). He was not condemning human affection. He commended our human loves and our love for self if exercised with a love for others. He was saying that even the closest, warmest commitments of our lives are superseded by a devotion to God. His expression was purposefully extreme to make the point. These are the perennial conflicts in commitment —between our loyalty to God and to our business, the state, the family. Commitments are multiple for us and drag us in many directions.

There seems to be a rebellion on the part of many against commitment in general, a mood of detachment which makes us want to be free of all obligations. Commitment may be painful. There are relatives who make demands, a state that makes requirements which are repugnant to us, business firms which ask for labor beyond our strength. We pledge ourselves. The burden becomes too great and we would like to be free.

We are sometimes disillusioned with the institutions in which we have put our trust. A labor union member thinks that the officials of his union have let him down. An unemployed person has lost trust in his government to provide a solution to his need for work. An elderly person feels that he has been forgotten by a nation that leaves him in want. A church member thinks that the church has nothing to say to his particular problem. Another feels the church has let him down by taking a certain position. Institutions are seen by these folk as self-serving rather than people-serving. Disenchantment has set in.

Or there are those who are afraid that commitments will deprive them of their freedom to do as they please. Their theme song is an old one, "Don't fence me in!" "Sit loose," is their advice. "Don't be tied down! Don't let anyone take you in!" Of course resistance to commitment of all kinds has its effect on our religious loyalties.

There are hundreds of detached people on the rolls of our churches. Once they were interested, involved in church activities, making a contribution to the church's life. Now they are names on the roll. Some have substituted other organizations and causes, but some, like one I visited recently, are lonely, lacking in purpose outside the gratification of their own desires. This young person was at loose ends. Unmarried, not involved in anything that required something from her, she was losing interest in life. If we are not obligated at all, if we are unwilling to entrust ourselves and what we have to others and to God, then we can only be committed to ourselves, to do "our own thing." The circle of our own interests becomes increasingly small and barren of meaning.

This happened with a teen-age boy who grew up in a pleasant suburban community and joined a delinquent gang in the city. Asked why he did it, he explained, "This way of life I was convinced gave me what I wanted, including purpose and meaning." He needed, as we all do, to belong to something, to share in some common enterprise; but how unfortunate was his choice! A news story tells of the demand of a group of American Nazis to parade in a predominantly Jewish suburb of Chicago, torturing in spirit the people who live there. Evidently these people needed to belong to something and a hate group was appealing. The attraction of people to the "Moonies," Scientology, the Hari Krishna movement, or any other of the multitude of cults which seem so attractive tells of the same need.

A young friend a number of years ago had set his heart on belonging to a certain fraternity at the college he attended. Unfortunately, he was not chosen. It ruined his college years and had a lasting effect on his life. He needed to know that he was chosen, that others wanted him in their fellowship, and he was frustrated that it did not happen. There is a need for a call to something in which we can invest our lives, satisfying a desire to be needed.

An officer in the church in a small city was a faithful servant of the church, a teacher and leader of youth; but something was missing. His business, which took most of his time, gave him no sense of meaning. He felt that he had talents which could be invested in a better fashion. In his middle years he made a venture of faith by selling his business, going to a theological seminary and later becoming an effective minister in a local church. Commitment brought for him meaning to his life.

Meeting the need of the individual is important, but our Christian commitment must go beyond that. A friend once said to the writer Turgenev, "It seems to me that to put oneself in second place is the whole significance of life." Turgenev replied, "It seems to me that to decide what to put before oneself in the first place is the whole problem of life." Loyalty to Christ comes first. Nothing can come before that. Commitment to his work is a primary obligation. Happily it is fulfilled in so many ways, according to the gifts which have been given to us. "Having gifts that differ according to the grace that is given us, let us use them" wrote Paul to the Romans (12:6), listing some of the many abilities entrusted to us. The work to which we are called is not usually some dramatic battle against a formidable evil, but rather a quiet, sometimes tedious, unglamorous series of efforts to demonstrate the love of God in action. The glorious thing about it is that losing ourselves in service we find ourselves. Jesus said, "Whoever would save his life will lose it, and whoever loses his life for my sake will find it" (Matthew 16:25).

A friend found this to be true. He retired rather early from his job with a large corporation. He had administrative ability, good health and a restless urge to do something important. He volunteered to be the superintendent of home missions in New Orleans Presbytery, looking after the interests of the small, dependent churches in that area, finding them pastors, seeing that they received help. He was also the home mission treasurer of the Presbytery. He agreed to do all this, a full-time work, without any salary or expense account. He gave over fifteen happy years to the task. He lost himself in the work to find himself, to gain a meaning for living.

One does not have to be an affluent executive to do this. When I went to one city church I found the plumbing in the manse needed repair. The secretary of the church said that the maintenance man would take care of it. I found later that he was a volunteer, a retired engineer who served without remuneration. For years he repaired whatever needed care in the church. When he became feeble another engineer took his place under the same arrangement. Neither asked anything from the church except an opportunity to serve. Both took delight in fixing ailing furnaces, defective plumbing and whatever else went wrong. A host of people of the same persuasion come to mind: a man who cares for the audio-visual equipment of the church, women who prepare and serve the meals in the church kitchen, the young people who painted the drab rooms of a classroom building, so many teachers, workers with youth, choir members, and people who work with alcoholics, who teach others to read, who carry hot meals to shut-ins, who work with poor children in recreation. The list goes on and on. How would Christ's church survive without commitment?

The work of Christ in the world faces challenges. It is up against entrenched oppression, the vast needs of hungry, impoverished and sick people, multitudes without faith or hope. The question persists, "How shall they hear without a preacher, and how shall he preach unless he be sent?" The answer to that question lies with committed Christians who support the church at home with all its activities as well as the work of the church far away, its schools and hospitals, its work among the oppressed and the needy.

Paul wrote to the Romans (12:1): "I appeal to you therefore, brethren, by the mercies of God, to present your bodies as a living sacrifice, holy and acceptable to God, which is your spiritual worship." When we despair over our inability to commit ourselves sufficiently to meet the need we must remember that we are dependent on "the mercies of God." Any commitment we make is grounded in God's all-out commitment to us. His prior commitment to us supplies the power we lack and indicates the manner and spirit in which we shall fulfill our obligations to him. As Christ gave everything for us on the cross, so we obligate ourselves for him. Out of our faith in him we receive the power to give of ourselves. He bridges the yawning gap between our promises and our obedience, forgiving, recalling, giving further opportunity. It is a continual process, a matter of committing ourselves over and over again in constant dependence on the source of our strength. Our commitment to him becomes a living force affecting all our actions. It is a liberating experience. We are freed from our false commitments as we are claimed by a true one.

Never underestimate the magnitude of Christian commitment, or its high cost. Jesus said, "If any man would come after me, let him deny himself and take up his cross and follow me" (Matthew 16:24). As Christ's commitment was dangerous, exposing him to rejection, pain and death, so ours may be. It may mean exposure to criticism, hard feelings.

A dedicated teacher in the public schools of a city in which I served spoke to our ministers' group of the obstacles which she faced in teaching, the behavior problems and particularly the lack of cooperation from the homes. Much of the trouble came from children who lived in miserable houses in a poor neighborhood. It happened that the pastor of a church that served a number of those homes was present. He rose to his feet and said, "Something must be done to get the families of those children to cooperate. I shall go to those homes and reason with those parents." Any pastor who has had to talk to parents about the behavior of their children knows what he faced—trouble. Yet he took it upon himself. That sort of commitment grows out of a love inspired by God's love for us. Our commitment to Christ strengthens and inspires all our earthly commitments that grow out of love—of a pastor to his people, of parents to children, of husbands to wives and wives to husbands. We are here for the sake of others, not simply those who are necessary to our own well-being, but also the countless unknown souls whose fate is joined to ours in a common humanity.

In Graham Greene's novel *The Power and the Glory,* the principal character is a priest who is often drunk, who has fathered a child and who in many ways has been unfaithful to his calling. It is at the time of the revolution in Mexico, and in his province it is forbidden that a priest administer the sacraments. He flees the province to save himself. His imperfections cannot keep him from a feeling of obligation to go back and minister to a dying ruffian at the risk of his life. He goes back and gives his life. Ironically his love is not appreciated. He was committed to something larger than his own safety. Christ's dying for his enemies, for sinful humanity, gives us an example that we should include all men, regardless of who they are, in the circle of our commitment.

Robert Bolt's play *A Man for All Seasons* has been called one of the great religious plays of our time. It is the story of Thomas More, the chancellor of England who refused to lie and say that he approved the divorce of Henry VIII from Catherine of Aragon, his marriage to Anne Boleyn and his subsequent declaration that he was the head of the Church of England. More remained silent and brought the king's wrath and imprisonment and death for his chancellor. One of the most moving scenes of the play is the visit of More's family to his prison cell in the Tower of London. He explains to his daughter Margaret that he must stand fast for the sake of all that is right and good for his people, for convictions that had grown out of his faith in Christ. Margaret exclaims emotionally:

> But in reason! Haven't you done as much as God can reasonably *want?*

He answers:

> Well—finally—it isn't a matter of reason; finally it's a matter of love.

This is the heart of the matter. Our commitment grows out of the love of God for us. It finds realization in our response, in our love for others and for him.

CHAPTER TEN

The Future Belongs to God

My wife had mentioned one morning that she was going to her doctor for a checkup, but I thought nothing of it, since she is accustomed to routine examinations. When she was late arriving home I grew worried. She came in just before the dinner hour and I knew in a moment that something was bothering her. She told me at once that the doctor had found an abnormality in her right breast and had called in a surgeon for consultation. She was to go into the hospital the next day for a biopsy to determine whether a major operation was necessary.

She had noticed her trouble on Monday (this was Wednesday) and had gone to the library and read a book which said that this could be a sign of cancer. Naturally, she was frightened. She made a doctor's appointment for Wednesday afternoon, but waited until she had the facts before telling me about it. She is an avid tennis player and had a match Wednesday morning. She said later that she played as if this were her last opportunity and won both sets!

I am an imaginative person and I had great difficulty sleeping Wednesday night. Facing the problem of a possible mastectomy and a long and perhaps fatal illness unnerved me. She had had a sister who had a radical operation of this kind a few years ago, so I knew all that was involved. The thought of her suffering and possible death was hard to bear. We have so much to live for—a fine family, plans for work and travel together, a wonderful companionship and a deep love for each other. Over and over that night I prayed,

"O Lord, don't let it happen!" and "Spare us this blow!" In our better moments we prayed that God would make us equal to anything that might come, that we would have the faith and courage to fight it. We have always believed that it is not so much what happens to you that matters but what you do with it. This was the opportunity to test the reality of our beliefs.

Entering a hospital requires so many routine tests that some of the anxiety was absorbed in the round of X-rays, shots, blood examinations, etc. This did not keep anxiety from hanging over us like a dark cloud until the appointed time came on Friday morning. I kissed her good-by at the door to the operating room and sat down to wait for news, good or bad. In a relatively short time the doctor came out to bring the good news that in his opinion the tissue was benign and that our worries were over. I was able to give my wife this assurance when she awakened a short time later. We rejoiced and gave thanks to God that she had been spared. Going through such an experience of fear and threat to life made us more able to identify with those who face similar experiences.

What if it had turned out the other way? So many of our friends have had that misfortune. We had one resource regardless of what came—hope. Of course, many have survived malignancies. Medical science has made many great strides, and we are grateful to God for what has been achieved. But where would we have been without the hope that faith supplied? Someone might say, "Hoping for a good report does not change the nature of the tissue from malignant to benign." Of course not. The real question concerns the spirit of those involved, the gift of a strength that is equal to any trial, the faith, however weak, that God cares, that the future belongs to him.

That sort of hope has sustained us through many situations—the birth of our children, several serious operations and other crises as well. It was our constant companion when one of our sons stood before the door of a church with his black friends asking for admittance in a time of tension and danger in the sixties. Hope enabled us to avoid despair when an opportunity to go to a very attractive and challenging church was ruined by an illness which quickly passed, but discouraged a calling committee. Later we came to the conclusion that our lives would have lost a great deal if that call had come through. How many experiences and relationships we would have missed if our wishes had been fulfilled then! How different our whole family would have been, probably different marriages for our children, opportunities for service missed. Looking at it with the perspective of the years, we would not change a thing. Through all that has happened to us we have had the assurance of hope that God had a purpose and plan for us, that we were always in his care.

We are creatures of hope. It makes us people of the future. A notice appeared in our daily paper this week: "Explorer of Life, Fred Noble, Dies at 94." The article described Mr. Noble's life, how he spent long years exploring everything this world had to offer. He was a quite successful practicing attorney, but his interests were endless—education, travel, the study of languages. He taught Greek, was fluent in German and Latin and was studying French at the time of his death. At eighty-four he earned a degree in history, at ninety a degree in teaching. He gave up tennis in his late sixties to take up mountain climbing. At ninety-three he took up flying! He taught Sunday School classes for over fifty years. He was a man who looked to the future, a man of hope. Most of us are not so gifted in body or mind as Mr. Noble, but traces can be found. I visit an elderly invalid in a nursing home who entertains the fantasy that she is going to return to her home—an impossible dream for her—but perhaps it keeps her alive.

Life is sterile and bitter without hope and sometimes it is in short supply. This is one of the tragic aspects of the nursing homes I visit. There is no goal or purpose for these older people. Many have lost connection with the future, the past and with reality itself. They need someone to bring meaning to their lives. The loss of hope is not confined to the elderly. Two young men came to my office recently asking for food for themselves and their families. We did what we could to help. I remembered that the same two had been by some months before. They admitted this. They were drifting, subsisting on handouts, with no future, no hope.

They were representative to me of many of the hopeless people of this earth, caught in a cycle of poverty, poor education, joblessness and sometimes their own unwillingness to face reality and to use the resources provided to build a satisfying life. There are millions in the world who lack the resources open to the young people who came to me, who have little hope of escaping their prisons of poverty and oppression. Refugee camps, prisons where torture is practiced and the prospect of millions without food or medical attention appall us. There is a mood of despair in the world, sometimes evident in the fears of people who hold onto their possessions and refuse to help, sometimes in the angry and frustrated people who turn to acts of senseless violence in their lack of hope that anything good will come. What hope has Christianity to offer to such a world? Is our hope valid?

Our hopes are mingled with our desires in such a way that we find it difficult to distinguish between the two. Is hope merely wishful thinking? Bertrand Russell thought that this was so. He said that life could be built adequately only on the basis of unyielding despair. Sigmund Freud thought that our hope was a disease, a refusal to face reality. He entitled an attack on the Christian faith *The Future of an Illusion*. Naturally, the person who fails to face reality has little chance of building a stable, constructive life, but nothing can be built on despair. There is a difference between wishful thinking and the hope on which Christians build their lives. Wishful thinking has nothing to support it. It is the vague feeling of a Micawber (in Dickens' *David Copperfield*) that something good is always just around the corner. Hope is not be confused with the gambler's desire to win. It has foundations. It is grounded, as we shall see, in history, in life-giving experiences.

There is nothing new in doubts concerning the value of hope. Pessimism dominated the thought of ancient Greece and Rome. Humanity, they thought, was headed for disaster. Hope was misleading. To illustrate, the Greek historian, Thucydides, gave this verdict:

> Desire and hope are never wanting, the one leading, the other following, the one devising the enterprise, the other suggesting that fortune will be kind, and they do immense harm, for being unseen they far outweigh the dangers which are seen. (*Peloponnesian War*, III, par. 45)

So hope was best distrusted. It would lead people astray. It would promise what never could be realized and so disappoint. The ancients thought the best solution to human problems was to face them realistically with resignation to despair. About the best advice the Roman Horace could give to his friend Albius Tibullus in a letter was:

> In the midst of hope and care, in the midst of fears and disquietudes, think every day that shines upon us the last. (*The Epistles of Horace,* Book IV, line 12)

Not too encouraging! It was little wonder that Paul could remind his Gentile friends at Ephesus:

> ... remember that you were at that time separated from Christ, alienated from the commonwealth of Israel, and strangers to the covenants of promise, having no hope and without God in the world. (Ephesians 2:12)

And he reminds them also: "You must no longer live as the Gentiles do, in the futility of their minds ... " (Ephesians 4:17).

In contrast to the hopelessness of the ancient world with its dark foreboding about the future, the Hebrews were forward looking. The element of promise is found in their earliest stories—of the creation, of Noah and the flood, of Abraham and the promises to his descendants, of the promise of a land to Moses and his people. The eleventh chapter of Hebrews gives a list of those who acted in faith on the promises of God, who, like Abraham, "looked forward to the city which has foundations, whose builder and maker is God." The Hebrews were characteristically a people of faith and hope. Their faith was defined as "the assurance of things hoped for, the conviction of things not seen."

The hopeful spirit in the Old Testament takes many forms. There is the hope for a Messianic age, for the coming of the "Day of the Lord," for the renewal of the whole earth. In the time of the Exile there was a hope for restoration and the vision of the Suffering Servant's meeting the deepest human needs. In times of repression and persecution the hope took an apocalyptic form, the destruction of the present order and the creation of a new one. Whatever the changing form or imagery of the expectation there was the underlying conviction that God's redemption was sure and that they should wait for it with patience. The psalmist expressed it in terms of the meeting of human need:

> For the needy shall not always be forgotten,
> and the hope of the poor shall not perish for ever.
> (Psalm 9:18)

For one psalmist it was hope without limits, "the hope of all the ends of the earth and of the farthest seas" (Psalm 65:5). No book of the Bible presents more poignantly the agony of the human spirit than the book of Lamentations, yet the writer says:

> The steadfast love of the LORD never ceases,
> his mercies never come to an end,
> they are new every morning;
> great is thy faithfulness.
> "The LORD is my portion," says my soul,
> "therefore I will hope in him."
> The LORD is good to those who wait for him,
> to the soul that seeks him,
> It is good that one should wait quietly
> for the salvation of the LORD. (Lamentations 3:22-24)

This same hopeful spirit was carried over into the New Testament, which was written against a background of Old Testament prophecy and expectation. John Baillie in his book *The Belief in Progress* finds a change in the pattern in the New Testament. The hope and expectation remain but there is fulfillment in Christ. His followers live in a new age. They have much to learn, guided by the Holy Spirit, but their hopes have a foundation in the Christ whom they have known.

The early hymns of the church which Luke recorded in his gospel are songs of joyous praise concerning the great things God was to accomplish in Christ, the scattering of the proud, the putting down of the mighty, the feeding of the hungry, the forgiveness of sins. All were to come through Christ who came

> to give light to those that sit in darkness and in the shadow of death,
> to guide our feet into the way of peace. (Luke 1:79)

Matthew quotes Isaiah as saying concerning Jesus: "He shall proclaim justice to the Gentiles . . . and in his name will the Gentiles hope," giving the hope a universal application (Matthew 12:18–21). Christ fulfilled this hope. He inspired hope in his disciples. He chose men such as Matthew, a taxgatherer, therefore a cheat and an outcast in the eyes of his people, and led him to become a faithful disciple. He took a fearful man like Peter and made him a bold leader who went to jail and finally to his death rather than be unfaithful to his Lord. Jesus gave hope by treating all people as important in God's sight and capable of redemption. A woman of Samaria was reached in spite of barriers of race and religion and inspired to have faith. Christ awakened faith in a Canaanite woman of Sidon who had a sick daughter and fulfilled her hope in the healing of her child. He gave hope to the blind, the deaf, the lepers and all the sick who came to him. He encouraged the outcasts of society, the losers of the world to believe that they were important in God's sight. He taught his disciples to hope when he told them to pray, "Thy kingdom come, Thy will be done, On earth as it is in heaven" (Matthew 6:10). In his last hours he told his disciples that they would be scattered and would leave him alone. "Yet I am not alone," he said, "for the Father is with me. I have said this to you, that in me you may have peace. In the world you have tribulation; but be of good cheer, I have overcome the world" (John 16:32–33).

The revelation of God's love in Jesus Christ is the source of our hope. Christ's coming into the world in human form, his life of loving service among us, his sacrificial death for our sakes all offer to us a confident hope. It is because God has shown that he cares with a depth of love beyond our comprehension that hope is possible for us.

Faced with the death of his friend Lazarus, Jesus amazed his followers with the proclamation, "I am the resurrection and the life; he who believes in me, though he die, yet shall he live, and whoever lives and believes in me shall never die" (John 11:25). He encouraged faith in that promise by restoring Lazarus to life, but the fulfillment of the promise was in his own Resurrection. We can imagine the weakness of his followers, a tiny band pitted against the hostility of the authorities and the might of the Roman world. They demonstrated often their lack of vision, their misunderstanding of Christ's mission, their insufficient faith. The Resurrection changed all that. They became a zealous, courageous, hopeful group of people who turned the world upside down. The Resurrection was their greatest stimulus to hope, a transforming event which made devoted disciples out of frightened followers.

Evidently Paul did not know Jesus during our Lord's life on earth. After his death he persecuted the members of the early church with zeal. This was all changed when he received a vision of the living Lord on the road to Damascus. From a man who despaired of salvation, of achieving any goodness in life, he became a person with a confident hope in Christ's saving power. Instead of condemning Christ and his followers he became the most articulate voice of the Christian church. A man narrow-minded and dogmatic, a man who never looked beyond the confining wall of his own heritage became the apostle to the Gentiles and welcomed the whole world into the Christian fold. To Paul the Resurrection was so powerful, not only in its assurance of a life to come but also in its renewing of life in the present, that he longed to be one with Christ that he might share his Resurrection. He made it the heart of his preaching and writing. He found the Christian faith inconceivable without it. He wrote to the Corinthians: "If Christ has not been raised, then our preaching is in vain and your faith is in vain" (1 Corinthians 15:14). Christ's Resurrection became for him the assurance of the rising again of all humanity who belong to him: "In Christ shall all be made alive" (1 Corinthians 15:22). The power of the Resurrection in Paul's life is one of the strongest witnesses to the transforming influence of Christian hope. Paul's experience does not stand alone, however. People are being renewed by hope all the time. It does not have to be a spectacular experience.

One of the most hopeful persons I have known was a woman who grew up in very limited surroundings. She told me that the home of her parents on the edge of a swamp was often engulfed with water in the rainy seasons, that there was little money, few clothes, not much encouragement for a girl with high hopes for life.

But nothing embarrassed her. The dignity and good sense she always displayed made her respected by all. She was a loving and devoted mother, an understanding wife, and excellent teacher. She seemed to think and act with Christian insight in almost every case. This woman was very ill, suffering greatly, often in the hospital, yet never complaining, never discontented with life. She told me often that she was quite ready for death or anything that God had in store for her. She was able to believe that "in everything God works for good with those who love him" (Romans 8:28), that no peril could separate her from the love of God, that "in all these things we are more than conquerors through him that loved us" (Romans 8:37). She inspired hope in others.

Sue illustrated in her experience what Paul said about the development of hope. He wrote to the Romans concerning the peace we have with God through Christ, the grace of God that sustains us, the hope "of sharing the glory of God," and then continues:

> More than that, we rejoice in our sufferings, knowing that suffering produces endurance, and endurance produces character, and character produces hope, and hope does not disappoint us, because God's love has been poured into our hearts through the Holy Spirit which has been given to us. (Romans 5:3–5)

It is normal to find trouble and suffering in life. Unfortunately, pain does not always produce endurance or result in a strong and steadfast character. It is often too much for us. It may embitter or destroy us, and often does. It did not have that effect on Sue. Her experience of the love of God and her confidence that he had a purpose for her produced endurance and, in turn, a character of unswerving integrity. The result was a victorious hope. There is something which we can learn from her that may help us to find hope too. The love she learned from God was exercised in her relationships with others—her family, her friends, her fellow church members. Hope and love were inseparable. There is a vital connection between "faith, hope and love," the abiding realities which Paul named in 1 Corinthians 13:13. They belong together.

Recently a successful businessman in Alabama volunteered at

the age of fifty-nine to go as a Peace Corps worker to the Philippines. He worked in a rural bank and encouraged the poor people of that country to improve their farming through loans. He lived on the salary of a Peace Corps worker, $125 a month, sharing much of the deprivation of the people for eighteen months and being away from his family for that period. He had worked all his life money-motivated, but his values changed as he was able to help people and know their love. He described it as kin to a religious experience in which "self-knowledge, self-esteem and feelings of unity with mankind" were found. He described himself as ready for "other mountains in the future." In caring hope was created, for others as well as himself.

The hope we have in a resurrected, living Christ, active in our lives now, opens the door to the future for us. We are liberated from doubts and fears to live in anticipation of God's redemption of all the world. Sometimes we "groan inwardly" as we wait, as Paul expressed it in Romans 8. The hatred and violence of human beings seem to make a monstrous denial of the hope of a renewed life that we have in the Resurrection. It is hope that is not seen, as are all our hopes, but still "we wait for it with patience." But we do not wait with folded hands.

The hope we have in Christ is a gift. It must be received in childlike faith. We receive it as we act in love, as we work for justice for all human beings, as we minister sacrificially to human need, as we labor to build peace and brotherhood. Wherever Christ's words are heard and heeded, "as you did it to one of the least of these my brethren, you did it to me," there hope is present, a hope for all mankind.